INCREDIBLE
FISHING
STORIES

INCREDIBLE FISHING STORIES

By Shaun Morey

Illustrations by Jared Lee

WORKMAN PUBLISHING · NEW YORK

Fish trivia from the International Game Fish Association,
*The Guinness Book of Animal Facts & Feats, Age of Fishes, The Life of
Fishes, The Fishes, Ways of Fishes, A Natural History of Sharks, The
Ocean World*, the National Marine Fisheries Service, and the National
Oceanic and Atmospheric Administration.

Library of Congress Cataloging-in-Publication Data
Incredible Fishing Stories: actual tales by real anglers / collected,
personally verified and written by Shaun Morey.
p.   cm.
ISBN 1-56305-637-2 (paper)
1. Fishing—Anecdotes.   I. Morey, Shaun.
SH441.I53   1994
799.1—dc20   94-1329
CIP

Workman books are available at special discounts when purchased
in bulk for premiums and sales promotions as well as for fund-raising
or educational use. Special editions or book excerpts can also be
created to specification.
For details, contact the Special Sales Director at the address below.

Workman Publishing Company, Inc.
708 Broadway
New York, NY 10003

First printing June 1994
Manufactured in the United States
10 9 8 7 6 5 4 3

DEDICATION

To my mother, Patti, who placed a fishing rod in my hands when I was two years old and who continues to be the most determined angler I have ever known.

To my father and favorite fishing buddy, Carter. Zings and dings, may it never end.

To my brother, Drake, to whom I owe so much. He is my traveling companion, my motivator, my first mate and my best friend. I could not have completed this book without him.

And, most important, to my wife, Alison. She believed in my dreams, encouraged my hopes and inspired me with immeasurable confidence. She is my ship, my compass and my true love.

CONTENTS

PART II

GRUELING BATTLES

PART III

REVENGE OF THE FISH

PART IV

LEGENDS, RECORDS AND MYTHS

INTRODUCTION

My fishing life began in earnest as a teenager surf fishing the tidal flats of Rocky Point, Mexico. The sun had set when a large and mysterious fish yanked my fishing rod from its holder, hurled it down the beach and carried it into the surf. The next morning as I stalked the shoreline for schooling fish, I spotted the rod washed up on the sand. It was as if the fish was taunting me, daring me to try again . . .

Incredible Fishing Stories is a collection of fishing's most memorable events: Dave Romeo's world record catch of 3,001 largemouth bass in three months; the standoff between a fishing boat and a naval destroyer that led to the first 1,000-pound blue marlin caught in the Pacific Ocean; Bob Smith's lifelong quest to catch every species of North American wild trout.

The collection includes remarkable catches like the two 12-pound largemouth bass landed with a single lure; the 1,600-pound hammerhead shark subdued with a handheld Hawaiian sling; and the marlin caught from a surfboard.

There are hard-fought battles that test both fisherman and fish, like Bob Ploeger's 37-hour duel with a record salmon on Alaska's Kenai River. And there are harrowing tales of fish attacks, of anglers going overboard and of danger from other fishing creatures—a rattlesnake in pursuit of a boat, a brown bear hungry for hooked salmon, a notorious crocodile named Sweetheart.

You'll read about unusual hook-ups like the feeding bat caught on a fly and the vicious alley cat that prowled too close to the water. You'll learn how an angler's severed thumb was recovered from the gutted belly of a mackinaw trout and why a satchel of money was caught instead of a walleye.

This collection represents 10 years of interviewing captains and anglers, compiling photographs and video tapes, corroborating each incredible account. During that time I logged thousands of miles tracking stories from Alaska to Australia, from Mexico to the Caribbean, from the East Coast to the West. Along the way I met hundreds of fascinating people. It has been a remarkable experience.

Today, my search for stories continues. If you have an incredible fishing story, or know of one I should investigate, send me a brief explanation. Include a return address and a telephone number where I can contact you.

And continue to help our sport grow. Include kids in your next fishing trip. Teach them a new knot. Tell them your favorite fishing stories. Without a new generation of fishermen, our sport is doomed.

Keep in touch, and fisherman's luck always!

Shaun Morey

INCREDIBLE
FISHING
STORIES

REMARKABLE CATCHES

BEAR CATCH

For more than 30 years Dr. John Craighead has studied bears. He is the world's leading expert on bear behavior, and he is credited with pioneering the practice of capturing, color-marking and radio-tracking bears. Craighead is also an avid fisherman, so it was no surprise that this world-renowned bear expert caught a bear on rod and reel.

It was summertime in Alaska, 1980, and Craig-head and his daughter Karen stood near a waterfall on the shore of the Brooks River. They were there to observe brown bears gathering at the falls to feed on migrating salmon. On this morning no bears were present, so the Craigheads spent the free time fishing for their daily dinner of sockeye salmon.

"We were fishing a spot where the brown bears aggregate to catch salmon," Craighead said. "The

Courtesy Karen Craighead

Dr. John Craighead tussles with a brown bear that emerged from the trees along the Brooks River in Alaska to take the salmon he had caught moments earlier. The bear was attracted by the thrashing fish and the clatter of Craighead's reel.

salmon move up the Brooks River and are temporarily stopped by a falls. This makes the salmon more readily available to the bears and provides many opportunities for us to observe them."

Craighead quickly caught two salmon and was playing a third when, on the opposite side of the river 100 yards down current, he saw a brown bear emerge from the timber. The bear entered the water and forded the river.

"Over the years," Craighead said, "the local bear population learned that the sound of a splashing fish or a screeching reel meant an easy meal. The bears would approach a fisherman, usually a tourist from another country, who would then drop his pole and retreat into the alders, leaving the fish he had caught lying on the bank."

> **❝I had the bear on for 30 seconds or more, but of course there was nothing I could do. When the bear reached the bank, I tightened the drag and broke the line.❞**

As Craighead played his salmon, the bear exited the river and ambled toward him and his daughter. Concerned that the bear would smell the two fish lying at his feet, Craighead told Karen to wrap the fish in a plastic bag and place them inside his backpack.

"At the spot where I was fishing," Craighead said, "the water was about 20 feet deep. Behind me the vegetation of spruce and alder was impenetrable, so the only way out was along the bank toward the bear. I told Karen to stand behind me and get her camera ready because I thought she might get some interesting pictures."

Craighead's salmon had jumped a few times but remained well downstream. The bear continued along the bank, then suddenly plunged into the river 75 feet from where the Craigheads stood.

The bear swam after the hooked salmon, pawed it, and turned back toward shore. Craighead's rod bowed forward and line pulled from the reel.

"I had the bear on for 30 seconds or more," Craighead said, "but of course there was nothing I could do. When the bear reached the bank, I tightened the drag and broke the line."

The bear entered the heavy brush and began to eat the freshly caught salmon. The Craigheads quickly assembled their gear and started along the bank. Their only escape was downriver past the feeding bear.

"I wanted to get out of there," Craighead said, "before the bear finished the salmon and came after our other two fish. I knew we didn't have much time. As we passed the spot where the bear had disappeared, we could hear him feeding on our salmon."

Camp was a quarter-mile trek through dense spruce and alders. The Craigheads made record time.

"When the bear first appeared," Craighead said, "I felt certain that he was after something to eat. I didn't think he was in an aggressive mood or preparing to charge us. But bears are unpredictable. I'm thankful I had a fish on at the time, because we didn't have any escape route had he decided to come after the two salmon I had already landed."

TWO TROPHY BASS ON ONE LINE

It was a Father's Day that Mike Bledsoe will never forget. He and his eight-year-old son Jacob left home that June morning in 1993 for a day of bass fishing at Lake Casitas in Ojai, California. Just before daybreak, they slid their 16-foot aluminum bass boat into the water and drove across the lake to one of their favorite fishing spots.

They had been fishing for about an hour when Bledsoe cast his plug across a shallow point in the lake and began a slow retrieve.

"I had just started reeling when I got a hit," Bledsoe said. "It was a big fish, and it came clear out of the water. I went to set the hook and I missed him."

Mike Bledsoe and his son Jacob with the two trophy bass landed together on one line. The bass on the left weighed 12 pounds. The bass on the right weighed 11 pounds, 12 ounces.

Courtesy Mike Bledsoe

The plug fell from the fish's mouth and skidded across the water. Bledsoe quickly reeled in the excess line when the fish suddenly struck again.

"There was a huge splash," Bledsoe said, "and we could see the size of the bass. I thought I had him, because I felt the weight, but a few seconds after I set the hook the fish hit again. I turned to Jake and said, 'What am I doing wrong?' I had never experienced anything like that before."

Bledsoe set the hook for the third time, still uncertain whether he could hook the awkwardly behaving bass.

"That's when I really felt the weight," Bledsoe said. "The fish took off and never broke water again."

Bledsoe told Jacob to reel in his line and get ready to net a large bass.

"The bass fought hard," Bledsoe said, "but it wasn't the tremendous fight I thought it would be. There was more deadweight than anything."

Bledsoe hoped the bass weighed more than 10 pounds. He had caught many eight- and nine-pound bass before, but a 10-pounder was a trophy fish. He also wanted to fulfill his promise to Jacob, the promise to mount any bass that weighed 10 pounds or more.

Not until the catch was near the boat did Bledsoe see that two bass were hooked to the plug—one to the front treble hook, the other to the back hook. They were swimming in tandem, and both were large fish.

"When I saw how big they were, I backed off on the drag and let them run again. I didn't want to lose them."

After a short run, Bledsoe tightened the drag and eased the two bass to the boat. Jacob waited patiently, and then, with one swift scoop, netted both fish.

"Jake did a great job of getting the fish into the net," Bledsoe said. "He wasn't strong enough to get both of them into the boat, so I laid my rod down and we lifted them together. We were so excited, our knees were shaking."

They put the fish in the live well and returned to the lakeside for an official weight. One bass weighed 12 pounds even. The other weighed 11 pounds, 12 ounces. Both were trophy fish caught with one cast.

"We couldn't believe it," Bledsoe said. "All the way back to the dock, we kept opening the live well and looking at those two fish. Jake and I really wanted a 10-pound bass, but we never dreamed of catching two at the same time."

Today, the impressive double mount hangs on a wall in the Bledsoe home. The scene re-creates the moment of the strike. The first bass is hooked to the front of the plug. The second and larger bass, its mouth agape, hovers just below, preparing to strike from behind.

It is an ominous sight.

DID YOU KNOW?

The largest fish in the world is the whale shark. The fish can grow to more than 40 feet and weigh more than 20 tons.

WRESTLING A 1,600-POUND HAMMERHEAD SHARK

When Capt. Jim Lewis first entered the water, he had no intention of killing the shark. Not only was it the largest hammerhead he had ever seen, it was also longer than the boat.

Lewis was in the Bahama Islands enjoying a one-day break between fishing tournaments with his wife Holly and two friends, Rolando Encinosa and Andy Gill. It was early morning and their destination was Great Harbor Island, a snorkeler's paradise 50 miles to the north.

They had been traveling only 20 minutes when Lewis spotted what looked like the tail section of a small plane rising two to three feet above the water. Veering in for a closer look, they saw the mysterious tail section move and disappear beneath the water. Encinosa throttled the boat to full speed as Lewis ran to the bow and peered down into the clear water.

Fifteen feet below, swimming along the bottom of a narrow channel, was a huge hammerhead shark.

"Toss me a mask," Lewis yelled. "I'm going in!"

An experienced open-water diver, Lewis was confident that the swift current flowing through the narrow channel would confine the shark's movements. He slipped on the mask, clutched a short Hawaiian sling and plunged into the water.

"The shark was enormous," Lewis said afterward, "and he knew I was there. He would turn his head and roll back his eyes to look at me."

As his confidence mounted, Lewis dove deeper to study the shark. During one of his descents, he counted 19 remoras clinging to the shark's body and noticed several half-moon gaff scars along its side and back. The hammerhead was an old shark that had felt the sting of a hook many times before.

Lewis desperately wanted to hook the shark, but all his fishing gear was in Chub Cay. Only snorkel equip-

Left to right: Rolando Encinosa, Andy Gill, Holly Lewis and Capt. Lewis. Note the length of the dorsal fin and the bulging belly where the 110-pound lemon shark was found sliced cleanly in half.

Courtesy Capt. Jim Lewis

ment was readily available. And the Hawaiian sling.

"I knew my only chance was a shot in the gills," Lewis said. "The range of the sling was only five or six feet, so I had to get close. Still, I didn't know if it would be enough to stop the shark."

Lewis took a deep breath and kicked downward. His heart raced as he cocked the rubber band. He swam as close as he dared and fired. It was a perfect shot. The shark lunged toward Lewis, but it was no use. He had guessed right. The strong current had allowed him time to reach the surface.

He climbed onto the boat and hurried to the bow. But the shark was swimming faster than before, blood streaming from its gills.

"What are you going to do now, Tarzan?" Encinosa joked.

Lewis didn't answer. The channel was getting deeper and would soon empty in open sea. He uncleated the grapple anchor and its 30 feet of chain and yelled for Encinosa to drive ahead of the shark.

"It was all we had that resembled a hook," Lewis explained. "Rolando drove ahead of the shark, and I threw out the anchor and let it sink to the bottom. When the shark swam by, I tried to snag him with it."

But to snag a shark with an anchor proved nearly impossible. Holly, Lewis' wife, counted the attempts. On the 36th try, the shark jerked its head sideways and lunged at the anchor. Lewis pulled back, and miraculously the anchor slipped into its wounded gill.

Lewis held the chain and Encinosa put the engines into neutral. The shark fought valiantly, towing the boat along the channel. But eventually the wounded shark tired and Lewis was able to haul it to the boat. Holly and Gill rushed to lasso the shark's huge tail.

Suddenly the hammerhead came to life, spinning dangerously alongside the boat. The powerful tail spun like a propeller, slapping Gill back across the deck and into the console, where he lay stunned on the floor.

"It was a crucial moment," Lewis said. "The shark was alive and we didn't have a gun on board, so we had to ground him."

They pulled the shark into the shallow water near one of the flats and waited. When he could approach safely, Lewis loosened the tail rope and wrapped it around the shark's head for the trip back to Chub Cay.

At 3 o'clock in the afternoon, the small boat pulled up to the crowded dock. Onlookers watched as the Jaws-like shark was slowly raised from the largest scale in Chub Cay. But before the shark was fully aloft, the scale, reading 1,100 pounds, jammed and broke.

Fortunately, members of a University of Miami marine research team visiting Chub Cay were in the crowd. The marine biologists asked to take samples from the shark and offered to weigh it scientifically. Lewis gladly accepted the offer.

The shark was a great hammerhead. It measured 15 feet, 6 inches and had a girth of 10 feet, 3 inches. It weighed an incredible 1,475 pounds. The team from Miami also examined the catch from head to tail. In the roof of the shark's mouth they counted 19 stingray barbs, while in its bulging belly they found a 110-pound lemon shark. The lemon shark was freshly eaten, sliced cleanly in half, and when added to the shark's weight pushed the final tally to nearly 1,600 pounds—more than 600 pounds over the current all-tackle world record.

Capt. Jim Lewis and his wife Holly with the 1,600-pound, 15½-foot hammerhead shark that Lewis swam with and landed using only a Hawaiian sling and later a grapple anchor. Note the enormous head, nearly four feet from eyeball to eyeball.

Courtesy Capt. Jim Lewis

A Bat on a Fly

From Erie, Pennsylvania, Broken Straw Creek flows southeast into the Monongahela River and from there turns north and merges with the Ohio River. There are trout living in the creek, and in the spring when the flutter and buzz of interminable hatches of newborn insects swirl above the currents, the fly fishermen come and fill their creels with frenzied rainbows and browns.

❝I had just made a cast and the line was falling toward the water when a bat flew by and took the bottom fly.❞

Luther De Armitt fished Broken Straw Creek often. He was a local resident who honed his fly-fishing skills on the multitude of streams and creeks that tangle along the northern Pennsylvania hills.

In 1969, on an early spring evening, De Armitt stood in the water of Broken Straw, casting flies into the creek. He used a 3-fly spread on 5 feet of leader line, each wet fly spaced 15 inches from the other.

"It was almost dark," De Armitt said, "and I was throwing my flies upstream, letting them sink and move down with the current. I had just made a cast and the line was falling toward the water when a bat flew by and took the bottom fly."

The snared bat twitched and jittered, swooped and darted, in every direction, trying to escape the pull of the tiny fly hook.

De Armitt was in a sudden and unexpected predicament. He couldn't cut the fishing line without burdening the bat with a long tail of flies. And he couldn't unhook the bat without risking a bite and possible infection from rabies or some other horrid bat-carried disease. He didn't want to harm the bat, but he had no alternative. He was in pursuit of trout, not bats, and he wanted his three flies back.

"I didn't know what kind of bat I had hooked," De Armitt said, "but it wasn't a big one. As it flew around, I kept my finger on the spool, and since the bat didn't have the power to take any line out I was soon able to get it to the shore. It landed on the ground a few feet from where I was standing."

De Armitt placed his foot over the bat and quickly ended its suffering. He retrieved his fly and returned to fishing.

"I didn't think much of it at the time," De Armitt said. "I know bats catch flies, and this one must have been swooping up and down the river in search of food. It just happened upon my fly in midair."

De Armitt has fly-fished for more than 50 years. He's hooked many fish, some too large to land. But the bat was the most unusual catch of his fishing life—and it was the last thing he ever imagined would take his fly.

3,001 BASS IN A WORLD RECORD 77 DAYS

"One more for good luck," Dave Romeo shouted to the crowd lining the shores of Kahler's Pond, Long Island, New York. It was the afternoon of October 28, 1984, the last day of fishing season. Romeo, who had already caught 3,000 largemouth bass, flipped up the tip of his fishing rod and set the hook on his 3,001st. He played it for a few extra minutes, enjoying his moment of glory.

Mobs of media had joined the lakeside crowd to witness and record Romeo's final bass of the year. A smile stretched across Romeo's face as he bent down to release the fish. He had shattered all previous estimates of a single-season catch. Names like "Bass Master" and "the Babe Ruth of Bass Fishing" would become common sobriquets for this 25-year-old tax consultant.

But Romeo was not your average fisherman. He was devoted to, almost obsessed with, better fishing. He had devoted three years to studying the art of bass fishing, keeping a detailed record of every bass he caught including dates, times, locations, weather patterns, baits and lures.

"There had to be reasons for fish to bite," Romeo explained. "Certain days were better than others. My goal was to figure out why."

He read every bass fishing book available,

Three of the many largemouth bass caught by Guinness record holder Dave Romeo.

Courtesy Art Gardner

searching for new strategies and new techniques. The best advice came from Robert Deindorer's *Positive Fishing: The Art of Angling to Your Outer Limit*, whose central theme was concentration—the more you had, the more fish you would catch.

"I broke the 1,000 mark by June," Romeo said, "and knew I could double it by the end of the season. I wanted the people at Guinness to recognize the record, but they were hesitant. So I got on the phone and contacted everyone with a vested interest in the record. Every fishing company whose tackle I was using sent letters on my behalf. I also sent in all the media coverage I'd received to verify my claim to the record."

Fourteen hours every weekend day, every vacation day and every day off, Romeo searched for bass. He weathered the cold, the rain and the wind. He ate little, resting only to switch lures or change locations. Though a dedicated angler, he missed only one day of work the entire three-month season. Fishing from inflatable rafts, small boats and shorelines, Romeo averaged 38 to 40 bass a day for 77 days. All but 28 of the 3,001 fish were released; some were caught more than once, while one was caught more than six times.

Romeo became a hometown hero. He even wrote a book, *Better Bass Fishing: The Dave Romeo Way*, and founded a family-style catch-and-release bass tournament that bears his name.

One more thing. During his quest for the record, he met his future wife. Her name? Kim Trout, of all things.

SURFING FOR MARLIN

When Dr. Hal Neibling and Curt Herberts left the harbor at Mexico's famed Cabo San Lucas, little did they know they were about to make billfishing history—of a sort.

They were aboard Lee Stockland's sleek sportfisher *Tio Lee*, skippered by Randy Wood. It was 10 o'clock in the morning, and they were drift-fishing for marlin two miles from shore. Neibling

was fishing from the bow, Herberts from the stern.

Suddenly, both anglers hooked up. Herberts' fish crashed through the surface, leaping and splashing its way due south. Neibling's fish did the same, except it headed due north.

Wood didn't move the boat. Instead, he hurried down from the bridge and raced inside the cabin. He found the board portion of a Windsurfer carried for windy days, rushed out to the deck

Hal Neibling fights an estimated 150-pound striped marlin from the base of a Windsurfer miles from the coast of Cabo San Lucas, Mexico.

Courtesy Hal Neibling

and dropped it into the water. Seconds later Neibling scrambled over the transom, straddled the board and moved across the water in pursuit of his marlin. Wood hurried back to the bridge and reversed the engines, leaving Neibling alone on a narrow board moving across the sea by the force of an angry marlin.

> **66 Seconds later Neibling scrambled over the transom, straddled the board and moved across the water in pursuit of his marlin. 99**

Meanwhile, Herberts' fish was more than 300 yards away and still taking line. "I couldn't put much pressure on the 20-pound line," he said afterward, "but once we started to follow the fish, it turned and headed back at us. I quickly regained 100 yards of line and things were looking up. Except when we turned to find Hal and he was gone."

The marlin had pulled Neibling away from the *Tio Lee* and was towing him out to sea. A breeze had begun to blow, creating an afternoon chop, but Neibling, who was wearing a life jacket, calmly fought his fish. Several small *pangas* and Mexican sportfishers circled in the distance, keeping him within sight.

"Those people must have thought I was crazy," Neibling said, "but it was all pretty easy. I kept my feet in the water for balance, and the drag on the reel set loose. The marlin did most of the work, pulling me along, tiring himself out. The only frightening moment was when I thought about sharks. I decided to put my feet on top of the board, and I nearly capsized. Needless to say, it was the last time I thought about sharks."

As Herberts' fish neared the boat, Stan Grier, another angler on board the *Tio Lee*, scanned the horizon with binoculars and finally spotted Neibling more than a mile away. Herberts tagged his fish, and 45 minutes after leaving Neibling the *Tio Lee* returned.

Neibling's marlin, now exhausted, hovered 30 feet below the water. Neibling was elated. Everyone on the *Tio Lee* offered encouragement as he asked for the tagging stick. He pulled the marlin close to the board, seized the leader in one hand, tied the rod to a trailing rope and tagged the fish one inch ahead and two inches to the right of the dorsal fin. Herberts tossed him a pocket knife, and Neibling cut the leader. He paddled to the boat, climbed onto the deck and asked for the coldest beer in the cooler.

JAYWALKING CARP

Officer Alvin Yamaguchi of the California Highway Patrol parked his car in the middle of the flooded intersection. It had been raining for days in southern California, and many of the major thoroughfares were closed to traffic. Smaller roads carried the overflow, but these too were beginning to fill with water.

"It was late in the afternoon," Officer Yamaguchi said, "and the rain wasn't letting up. One of our freeways was under four feet of water and commuters were using Irvine Boulevard, which parallels the freeway. Rattlesnake Canyon Reservoir, a few miles up in the hills, had overflowed onto the Boulevard. I was dispatched in case the road flooded and the traffic needed rerouting."

Officer Alvin Yamaguchi (at left) hoists the 30-pound carp he wrestled from the flooded streets of Irvine in southern California.

Courtesy Alvin Yamaguchi

When Yamaguchi arrived, Irvine Boulevard was a foot and a half under water. Vehicles were stalled and traffic was clogged for miles. Large chunks of debris floated down the middle of the 100-foot-wide road. Yamaguchi and his partner donned their rain suits and stepped into the submerged intersection to divert the tangled traffic.

"I had only been standing in the intersection for a few minutes," Yamaguchi said, "when my partner started hollering at me to come over to the other side of the patrol car. I thought something was wrong, and I ran around the car to see what was happening. My partner was pointing at a fish, yelling, 'It's a bass! It's a bass!'"

Yamaguchi looked to where his partner was pointing. A large fish was splashing its way down the middle of the road. Yamaguchi waited until the fish floated by, then reached down with both hands and scooped it into his arms.

"It was a 30-pound carp," Yamaguchi said, "and I didn't know what to do with it. I had it in a bearhug, standing knee-deep in the middle of the intersection. All I could think to do was handcuff it to the bumper of the patrol car."

He located a pair of plastic flex-cuffs and secured one end through the carp's mouth. The other end he cinched to the car's bumper. Motorists driving by waved and laughed at the unusual sight. Others called their local police departments.

"The word traveled fast," Yamaguchi said. "My fellow officers started calling on the radio to confirm the rumor. Nobody could believe it. The carp had come all the way down from the Rattlesnake Canyon Reservoir. Luckily, one of the city employees who was working at the intersection had a Polaroid camera and took a picture of me holding the fish."

The next day Yamaguchi gave the photograph to the police department's public affairs office for an article that had been written for the local newspaper. The story was sent by wire to papers across the country, and within days he was a celebrity.

"If I'd known all of this was going to happen," he said, "I would never have given the carp away. I would have taken it home and stuffed it."

Five months later Yamaguchi was contacted by the Bill Cosby company and within weeks he was flown to Philadelphia to appear on Cosby's game show *You Bet Your Life*. During the show, he recounted his unusual fishing story and in the process won $13,500 dollars in prize money. It was one of the largest wins in the show's history.

"I'm still surprised by all the interest it's caused," Yamaguchi said. "I always thought of carp as garbage fish, but not anymore."

OUT OF THE FRYING PAN INTO THE FIRE

On June 10, 1989, Bruce Hake was aboard the charter boat *Qualifier 105*, fishing near San Benedicto Island, 500 miles south of the tip of Baja, California. It was wahoo country. Clean, blue and deep.

Hake was fishing from the stern with four or five other hopeful anglers while the chum man, standing atop the bait tank, flung fresh anchovies into the sea. Schools of game fish circled the boat.

"I threw out my favorite wahoo jig as far as I could," Hake said, "and was reeling it in when my line went slack. Wahoo have razor-sharp teeth, so I thought I'd been bitten off."

But as Hake reeled in the slack line, a wahoo—with Hake's jig dangling from its mouth—shot out of the water 35 feet from the stern. The wahoo flew directly at the boat, and as Hake ducked, the fish soared over his head.

"I heard a splash," Hake said, "and when I turned around to see what had happened, there was my wahoo swimming in the bait tank with my jig still in its mouth!"

ESKIMO PIKE

It was five degrees below freezing on Sylvan Lake in Alberta, Canada, when Ernie Nagy arrived for a day of ice fishing. His four-wheel drive was stocked with the necessary gear: ice-fishing tent, ice auger, portable heater, thermos of hot coffee, sandwiches, bucket (for sitting and for holding the day's catch), rod and reel, and an assortment of hooks, spoons and fishing line. He had purchased the bait, a package of live maggots, at the corner store.

After drilling a hole through the three feet of surface ice, he slid the tent over the opening. The tent had a zipper door and a six-by-six floor of plywood with two holes cut through to allow access to the ice.

Nagy was looking for perch. "I was fishing a small handmade hook," he said, "wrapped in red-and-white telephone wire with a buckshot weight crimped near the eye. I baited the hook with two maggots and dropped it through the ice into approximately 25 feet of water, 6 inches off the bottom."

After an hour, he had caught only three perch. Leaving his line in the water and securing the rod to the bucket, he exited the tent and drilled a new hole near the shoreline.

"I returned to the tent," Nagy said, "and was just lifting my fishing rod when something hit with great force. I was so surprised, I nearly lost the rod."

The large fish dashed away beneath the water, dragging the delicate 6-pound line against the jagged lower edge of the ice hole. The reel was intended for smaller fish, and the drag system was inadequate for such a strong run. Nagy pressed his thumb on the spool to help slow the fish.

Forty feet away, the fish stopped. Carefully, Nagy began retrieving the line. He was concerned about the light line chafing on the ice and about the strength of the small homemade perch hook.

Courtesy Ernie Nagy

Ernie Nagy holds the 16-pound, 8-ounce northern pike he caught while ice-fishing at Sylvan Lake, Alberta, Canada. The pike was so large it became wedged in the small hole Nagy had cut in the ice.

Suspecting that the fish was a northern pike, renowned for bladelike teeth and fortitude, he knew his leaderless line would not last long.

"The hole I had cut was only six inches wide," Nagy said. "Even if I was lucky, and got the fish to the hole, I didn't think he would fit through."

Nagy wanted desperately to glimpse the fish, to confirm his speculations and to estimate its size. The water was clear, and he could see approximately 10 feet down. Three times the fish approached the 10-foot mark, and each time it stripped the same 40 feet of line from the reel.

"Each time I thought the line would break," Nagy said, "but somehow it held and finally the fish was close. I was kneeling down on the tent floor, anxiously peering into the hole and reeling cautiously, when suddenly there he was—a huge northern pike!"

The pike opened its jaws and turned on its side. Nagy's tiny red-and-white hook was firmly embedded in its lower lip. The pike was exhausted and hovered calmly beneath the hole. But still Nagy couldn't pull the large fish through the narrow shaft of ice with his fragile 6-pound fishing line.

At that moment, he remembered the large treble hook tied to a roll of 15-pound hand line stored inside his tackle box. He held the rod steady in one hand and reached into the box with the other. "The fish was still lying there with its mouth open, resting up for its next move, when I came up with the line. I dropped down the treble hook, and as it entered his mouth the pike snapped his jaws shut and took off straight down."

Nagy tossed the fishing rod aside and pulled up with both lines. The pike stopped, turned and began to cartwheel vertically 12 feet beneath the ice. Nagy waited patiently. He timed the pike's rotations, and then, as the fish made another upward turn, he yanked the lines with all his strength. The fish's momentum and the sudden tension on the lines brought the fish headfirst into the hole.

"I knew it was going to be a tight fit," Nagy said, "and maybe even impossible. I was still kneeling on the floor when the pike came full speed into the hole. He filled the entire space, and as he came up he forced two or three gallons of ice-cold lake water out of the hole and completely soaked me from head to toe."

The pike lodged in the hole with its head protruding a few inches above the surface of the ice, its rows of serrated teeth dangerously exposed. Nagy couldn't grab the pike by the mouth without risking a bite, so he took his "fish releaser," a four-foot section of bamboo pole used to shove any fish too small back down through the ice hole. He knelt beside the stuck pike, slipped the pole through the pike's exposed gills and with one firm yank pulled the fish from the hole. The pike horsewhipped wildly at the air. Nagy unzipped the tent door and flung the fish, the lines, and the rod and reel out onto the ice.

"I didn't want him flopping around in the tent with me," Nagy said. "Those sharp teeth can cause great damage to a careless angler. Just as I threw the pike out of the tent, a party of fishermen arrived and couldn't believe what they were seeing: a large pike flopping on the ice and a soaking-wet fisherman."

Nagy shivered with cold. He quickly packed his gear and drove to the corner store to weigh the pike. The scale registered 16 pounds, 8 ounces. It was the largest northern pike caught in Sylvan Lake that year.

DEAD BODY ON A FLY

Hal Janssen stood waist-deep at the mouth of the San Lorenzo River, where it flowed into northern California's Monterey Bay. He was fishing a slow-sinking fly line and a #10 orange-colored fly. The silver salmon had returned to spawn, and they were running thick that December morning in 1975.

"I had fished the river the weekend before," Janssen said, "and I knew the salmon were lying in the deep water near the steep bank where the river dumped into the bay. But on that morning the fish had moved upriver into very shallow water. It was unusual for the fish to be in such shallow water, and they weren't biting."

Unable to hook the shallow-water salmon, Janssen returned to the river mouth where the fish had been feeding earlier in the week. The other fishermen remained upriver, desperately trying to coax the schooling salmon to strike.

The tide was at its lowest and rising when Janssen waded onto the shallow sandbar and began casting toward the steep bank. After each cast, he allowed the fly line to sink seven or eight feet below the surface before beginning his retrieve. At about the sixth cast, he felt something catch the fly.

"All of a sudden I hooked something," Janssen said. "It didn't really move at the start, and when it did it moved slowly. I thought I'd hooked a large stringer of seaweed brought in from the bay."

Janssen pulled hard in an attempt to break the fishing line, but on each try the heavy object moved a few feet toward him. "I decided that whatever it was, I'd get it out of the water so no one else would get snagged. The river flowed right by an amusement park at the edge of Monterey Bay, and there was usually some sort of debris around. In fact, earlier that morning another fisherman had hooked a grocery cart."

The incoming tide helped push the heavy weight toward shore, and after four or five minutes of slowly working the reel Janssen saw the object emerge 30 feet away.

"I saw something brown that looked like the flipper of a seal. Commercial fishermen occasionally shot pesky seals, so I thought I'd snagged a dead one."

Janssen patiently retrieved the large object. It descended below the water and surfaced for the second time less than 20 feet away.

"This time I saw a bright pink color," Janssen said. "I kept pulling and the tide kept surging in, and the next moment there was this thing at the tip of my fishing rod. I pulled up hard to get a good look, and

I saw what looked like a manikin from a department store. I figured someone had robbed a local store and dumped a grocery cart and a manikin into the river."

Suddenly, a swell from the incoming tide lifted the object and dropped it beside Janssen's waist. The last thing he remembered was seeing the human body.

"I don't remember getting to the shore," he said, "but there I was, holding my fly rod and staring in disbelief at the body resting on the sandbar. The fly line was still attached, and I could see my orange fly."

An angler came around the bend and called out to him, but he was too discombobulated to reply. Then a second, more familiar voice called out from the levy above the bank of the river.

"A San Jose police officer who fished the river a lot and was a friend of mine had come down to see how the fishing was," Janssen said. "I had never been so glad to see a police officer in all my life. I told him what had happened, and he ran back to radio for help."

Janssen cut his fishing line and waited for the police to arrive. "I became an immediate suspect," he said. "The first thing the officer in charge wanted me to do was walk back into the river and retrieve the body, which was lying half-submerged on the sandbar. I told him I had dragged the body 85 feet across the river and that was as far as I was taking it."

Janssen steadfastly refused to retrieve the body so the policeman ordered another officer into the river. While the officer went to recover the body, Janssen answered questions and completed a report.

"I just wanted to leave," Janssen said, "but the police have their procedures. They told me I had to identify the body, which seemed ridiculous to me. I had described the clothing and told them where to find my orange fly, but they wanted me to physically look at the body and identify it as the one I had pulled in. I thought this was crazy. How many bodies did they think were lying in the river with an orange fly hooked to them? I was pretty upset about the whole experience."

Eventually, Janssen returned to the river and identified the body. He also identified his #10 orange fly that was hooked to the gloved hand of the victim.

Soon afterward, he was allowed to leave, but with strict instructions not to move out of state. "I was relieved to get out of there," he said. "I learned later that the victim was a local high school girl who worked at a nearby grocery store and had been missing for a couple of days. Her brown glove was what I thought was a seal's flipper, and the pink color I saw was the jacket she was wearing. She had been strangled, and a few weeks later a second body was found floating in the bay. It was a male, and in his wallet the police found a photograph of the girl.

"I never found out what had happened, and I was never called to testify at a trial, so I've always assumed the case was never solved."

"BRAZAKKA"

For over 20 years, Capt. Dennis "Brazakka" Wallace has fished one of the most magnificent stretches of water in the world—a place where the Pacific Ocean meets the Coral Sea, a place where 800-pound marlin are rats, and Big Julie, the elusive 2,000-pound black marlin, is only one strike away. The place is Australia's Great Barrier Reef.

A barrel-chested man with a bearded face and burgeoning belly, Brazakka is the epitome of a great fisherman. His successes have been many, including a running total of more than 60 1,000-pound marlin, 14 of them caught when he skippered for legendary actor Lee Marvin. My brother Drake and I met with Brazakka during the off-season at his deer ranch high in the Atherton Tablelands, 30 miles above the city of Cairns. An ascending ramp took us to the most unusual yet most pleasant office we had ever seen. It was perched high in the limbs of an ancient tree. The walls were covered with photographs of great fish, each with a memory of a great battle. And in the corners of the tree house were marlin bills the size of baseball bats.

Here are just a few of the stories he told that day.

BOTTOM FISHING FOR BILLFISH

The marlin season was still a month away when Brazakka fired up the twin engines of his boat and headed out the bay. The anglers on board had booked a one-day charter to bottom-fish along the shallow inner reefs.

Brazakka anchored the boat a few miles from shore above a clump of coral 20 fathoms deep. The anglers baited their hooks and dropped their handlines over the side. Table fish were their objective, and soon the eskees were bursting with red emperor and sea trout.

Brazakka rigged a handline and joined the anglers, and late that afternoon he caught the final sea trout. He unhooked the fish, tossed it into the eskee and waited for his guests to reel in their

Tagging a lively Australian black marlin.

lines. "While I was waiting," Brazakka said, "I decided to fix my line. It had become badly twisted, and before I could wrap it back on the spool it had to be straightened. I threw the heap of line out as far as I could away from the boat. There was nothing on the hook except a tiny bit of bonita skin."

Brazakka waited a few seconds before winding the line onto the spool. He had made a few turns when suddenly the line jerked forward, burning through his hands.

"At first I thought it was a shark," Brazakka said, "but the fish was too fast. I squeezed my hands around the line, and a small black marlin started jumping from the water. I couldn't believe it! Not where we were, and not on a bare hook."

But there it was, hooked and fighting hard to break free. Brazakka held the line taut and watched as the small billfish jumped itself to exhaustion. Then he hauled in the line, tagged the feisty minor and released it for another day.

"Maybe he'll be back," Brazakka said, smiling, "hopefully on the outside, hopefully as a grander."

FREE TAGGING A RAT

"Free tagging was great fun," Brazakka explained. "It was back in the '70s, when the fish were really thick. The small ones, 200- and 300-pounders, would play around the boat, and if one of them tried for our baits, we'd reel in as fast as we could.

"The playful marlin would follow the bait up to our stern, where the deckie would be waiting with the tag stick. If the marlin was close enough, the deckie would reach out and tag him.

"It was great fun! We tagged a lot of fish, and saved a lot of bait, too."

FOOD CHAIN

Brazakka and his deckie, Snudges, thought nothing of the flying fish breaking water near one of their trolled baits. Flying fish are a common sight in Australian waters.

And when a dolphinfish suddenly emerged, greyhounding in pursuit of the flying fish, the two men watched in amusement.

But when the water erupted with the fury of a hungry black marlin, Brazakka and Snudges were consumed with excitement. The dolphinfish scarcely had time to finish its meal when the marlin attacked.

"It was really something," Brazakka said, "watching it all happen so fast. The dolphinfish was so intent on catching the flying fish that it never had a chance. The marlin caught the dolphinfish by surprise, stunned it with his bill and speared it. The dead dolphinfish went belly-up on the surface with a hole right through its midsection."

The skillful marlin swallowed the dolphinfish and, still frenzied, turned toward the baits skipping behind the boat. Brazakka had begun to circle when a rod slumped and the reel sounded the strike. Two hours later the marlin was released with a tag in its flank.

"He wasn't that big," Brazakka said. "Eight hundred pounds, maybe more. But it was one of our strangest catches. To catch a marlin that had caught a dolphinfish that had caught a flying fish, one right after another like that, was extraordinary."

DOUBLE GIANTS

The weather was delightful on that Atlantic day in the early 1980s when one of Florida's most prominent professional skippers and tuna fishermen, Ed Murray, experienced his most unusual catch.

"We were tuna fishing out of Gloucester, Massachusetts," Murray explained, "and it didn't take long to catch our limit. But rather than quit for the day, we decided to continue fishing and practice our release skills."

Murray and his crew soon hooked a mega-tuna. The angler was patiently playing the large fish from the fighting chair when the fishing rod he was holding slumped forward and began to shake violently.

"My friend Don Stott was the one in the chair," Murray said, "and when the fishing rod bent over double and started shaking, we were confused and a little scared. I thought maybe an orca had come by and grabbed our tuna for dinner."

Stott's 130-pound test fishing line strained against the mysterious weight. Murray worked the boat and waited anxiously, expecting the line to snap at any moment. An hour passed when from beneath the cold, deep water emerged *two* giant tunas.

"The first 800-pound tuna was tail-wrapped about 20 feet up the double line," Murray said. "Another tuna of about the same weight was firmly hooked in the mouth. Both fish were alive, and we quickly released them unharmed. It was incredible, and none of us would have believed it if we hadn't seen it."

Two keepers caught by the Murrays during one of their many successful fishing trips.

Courtesy Capt. Ed "Cookie" Murray

RETURN OF THE CARP

Bob Lein and his wife Judy were enjoying a three-week fishing vacation in August, 1982, at the Hell's Canyon Recreation Area on the Idaho/Oregon state border. The area has three large reservoirs stocked with an assortment of prized game fish and covering hundreds of square miles. Rainbow trout, smallmouth bass, land-locked coho salmon, and sturgeon are some of the more coveted species.

Bob and Judy sat in their 14-foot aluminum boat on the Oxbow Reservoir, fishing for rainbow trout and coho salmon. They were anchored a few hundred yards from the Brownley Dam and had fished all morning. At midday, they took a lunch break. Judy reeled in her line and set it aside. But Bob, who hadn't had a strike since baiting his hook, left his line where it was and turned to enjoy his sandwich and converse with his wife beneath the sweltering summer sky.

"It was a perfect day for fishing," Bob remembered. "The turbines beneath the dam were shut down, and the air was still. I had set my rod down against the edge of the boat and wasn't paying attention when a fish hit and pulled the whole thing overboard. I heard the rod move, but it happened so fast I didn't have time to catch it."

Bob had several other rods in the boat and soon resumed fishing. "The rod and reel weren't very expensive," he said. "I was more disappointed about losing the fish than losing the gear. After a few minutes, I baited another line and fished the rest of the day, not giving it another thought."

A few days later Bob and Judy returned to the Oxbow Reservoir. They anchored downstream from the dam and on the opposite side of the reservoir. It was midmorning when Bob hooked a large fish. The fish hit hard, and at first Bob thought it was a large catfish. But as it neared the boat he saw the large scales and mottled color of a carp.

When he pulled the eight-to-nine-pound fish to the side of the boat and reached down to remove the hook, he noticed a second hook lodged in its lip. "There was fishing line attached to the second hook, so after I released the carp I started pulling in the extra line. I figured someone had broken a line during an earlier fight. Then I felt the line get heavy. I kept pulling, and pretty soon out from the water came the fishing rod I had lost three days before."

> **I heard the rod move, but it happened so fast I didn't have time to catch it.**

Bob carefully inspected the rod and showed it to Judy. They were both flabbergasted.

"Those turbines go off and on throughout the day and night," Bob said, "so the carp are pushed and pulled all over the place. It's hard to believe the rod and reel stayed attached to that line. And even harder to believe I could catch the same fish twice."

BEACHING A BILLFISH BAREHANDED

Hayden McDowell vaulted from the sand and ran toward the surf. A mysterious fin had appeared 30 feet from shore, knifing through the water toward his roommate's dog.

"I was sure it was a shark," McDowell said, "and Steve's dog was out there in the surf. It all happened so fast I didn't have much time to think about it."

McDowell and his roommate, Steve Bailey, were living on Sullivans Island, South Carolina, a small island near the entrance to Charleston Harbor. They had brought their dogs for a run along the beach when McDowell first saw the fin.

"When I got to the water, I saw it a second time and knew it wasn't a shark. I was curious and kept walking out deeper and deeper. When I got into chest-high water, the fish swam right by me, kind of slow. That's when I saw the bill and got excited. I figured it was a sailfish, so I just reached out and grabbed the fish by the tail."

As McDowell's fingers locked onto the base of the fish's tail, the startled creature lunged forward, pulling McDowell beneath the water. McDowell struggled to regain his balance, fighting to keep hold of the fish. He found a foothold in the sand and stood up, pulling the tail out of the water.

"I knew as long as I kept its tail above water, I could control it. I had to walk backwards and almost lost the fish once when the water rose above my chest, but I held on and when I hit the beach I was running.

"Steve came over and helped me drag the fish up on the sand. That's when I started jumping up and down. I kept yelling, 'It's a marlin! . . . It's a marlin!'"

McDowell and Bailey took the billfish by pickup truck to the neighboring Isle of Palms, where it was weighed and recorded by a representative of the local Game and Fish Department. The representative took measurements and tissue samples, and two days later announced a surprising discovery.

The samples identified the fish, not as a small white marlin, as first thought, but instead as a healthy female longbill spearfish. It was a fish that

DID YOU KNOW?

The shortest fish in the world is the dwarf pygmy goby. This colorless, nearly transparent fish lives in the lakes and rivers of the Philippines. A full-grown adult dwarf pygmy goby measures less than ½ inch.

Hayden McDowell (left), Steve Bailey and Bailey's dog Chappy with the 38-pound longbill spearfish McDowell caught barehanded from the surf off Sullivans Island, South Carolina.

Courtesy Terry Joyce

had never before been caught in South Carolina waters. The longbill spearfish weighed 38 pounds and measured 7 feet, 2 inches.

One year later a second longbill spearfish was caught off South Carolina, this time on rod and reel by angler Harry Johnson, confirming McDowell's claim to the discovery of a new species of game fish inhabiting the waters of South Carolina.

OVERBOARD WITH A SAILFISH

From his house overlooking the Pacific Ocean, Horace Witherspoon, trustee emeritus of the International Game Fish Association, talked about his life of fishing.

Witherspoon had been president of many fishing clubs, most notably the Avalon Tuna Club, Balboa Angling Club, Light Tackle Marlin Club and International Light Tackle Tournament Association. He had served on the IGFA board of directors for 30 years and played a fundamental role in the success of the first Pacific Ocean Game Fish Tagging Program. He was appointed by the governor of California to the U.S. National Marine Fisheries Advisory Committee at its inception in the early 1970s.

And, of course, Witherspoon fished, often.

"I haven't done anything extraordinary," he said humbly when I asked for an incredible fishing story.

"Nothing?" I asked, warily.

"Well, I suppose a few unusual things may have happened along the way."

Witherspoon hesitated. He didn't like to boast about his fishing. He had experienced much in his 80-plus years, but nothing worthy of a story. I stumbled around with words like "exciting," "unusual," "inspiring." Still nothing. Then, as my hopes for a fishing story dwindled, Witherspoon's wife, who had been sitting quietly nearby, spoke.

"Oh, Horace," she said. "Why don't you tell him about the time you fell off the boat in Mexico? You remember, when you were fighting that fish."

Witherspoon was stuck, and I had my story. Here's what he told me.

A number of years ago, I was fishing in a tournament about 20 miles off the coast of Acapulco, Mexico, with two other competitive anglers from the United States. The fishing was good, and we had a rule that in the event of a double strike, whoever hooked up first had control over the direction of the boat. I don't know if it was premonition or good timing, but just about then my good friend Frank Bivens hooked up.

Line was racing from his reel when I hooked up with a similar fish—a sailfish. Frank's fish was going away from the stern, while mine was heading away from the bow. So, fending for myself, I took the rod and worked my way forward along the gunwale. The skipper, meanwhile, was backing down the other way toward Frank's fish, which was jumping feverishly on the horizon.

My one obstacle along the way to the bow was the starboard outrigger. It had not been in use and was tucked vertically against the flybridge, so I reached out and grabbed it to pull myself along. I held the rod with one hand and the outrigger with the other, but as I leaned out and swung around, the outrigger pulled free and swung around with me—away from the boat and out over the water. I had nowhere to go but down!

The skipper stopped the boat, and everyone rushed to the gunwale to help me out of the water. But I refused their help. I knew if the catch was to be legal, nobody but the angler could touch the rod. A nearby boat had seen our predicament and knew we needed assistance. They came by and offered to take Frank aboard so he'd have a better chance at landing his fish. Frank knew I wasn't going to give in easily and gladly accepted the other boat's offer.

My sailfish, meanwhile, was fighting like mad, jumping across the surface and completely oblivious to my problems. I was worried about the line and the friction from the water, so I loosened the drag and hoped the line wouldn't break. I held the rod with one hand and kept myself afloat with the other.

A short time later I noticed the small porthole in the side of the boat. I could just reach it. I loosened the drag some more, swam over and jammed the rod into the hole. Then I climbed aboard the boat, ran to the porthole and pulled the rod back out. I tightened the drag and soon after reeled in the exhausted sailfish. I really hadn't thought much of it, but the third angler on board was overwhelmed with excitement. He congratulated me on a fine catch and gave me the T-shirt off his back as a memento. Mine was soaking wet, and I accepted it gratefully.

> **❝I knew if the catch was to be legal, nobody but the angler could touch the rod.❞**

Fifteen minutes later, Frank returned with his sailfish. Both our catches were legal and both qualified for tournament points.

We didn't win the tournament, but I still have that T-shirt. I saved it along with the swim fins and snorkel that were presented to me at the awards dinner that night.

THE KING AND THE KID

In the deep water of Lake Michigan lives the chinook, the king of the salmon family. Schools of these mighty fish roam the vast lake throughout the year until the primordial urge to spawn propels them into the smaller lakes and rivers that surround it. Although lake salmon do not compare in weight to the record chinooks of Alaska and Canada, many grow to an impressive size. In August, 1993, seven-year-old Champion Rankin landed one of the large ones, a king of kings.

Rankin and his dad were trolling diving plugs from downriggers from the stern of their 14-foot outboard fishing boat. They were on Père Marquette Lake, one of the many small lakes that surround Lake Michigan. Suddenly the rod bent and the water swirled beneath the fishing plug.

"I saw the fish's tail go up out of the water," Rankin said, "and I thought, *whoa!* That's a big fish."

Rankin's father grabbed the rod from the holder and handed it to his son, who gripped the rod firmly and struggled to end the fish's run. At age seven, Rankin was already an experienced angler. The two prior seasons he had accompanied his father in the search for salmon and had fought many himself. But this was the largest salmon yet, and he was determined to get it to the boat.

The salmon stopped and sulked deep in the cold water. Rankin leaned back with his entire body just to retrieve a few inches of line. The fish was well hooked, and after 20 minutes of ceaseless pulling Rankin's swivel struck the rod tip. His father reached over the side of the boat and grabbed the fish by the tail. The width of the tail was enormous, and his hands could scarcely surround it.

"Salmon have a bone tail," Rankin's father said, "so I don't carry a net. I wear fillet gloves that grip well, and I can usually pull a salmon on board with no trouble. But that was a big fish, and it was hard to get a good grip on his tail. I had to be extra careful not to drop him back in the water."

The salmon was stowed in the fish box and weighed hours later at a nearby tackle store. It mea-

DID YOU KNOW?

The largest sunfish ever recorded was run over by a boat 40 miles off the coast of Sydney, Australia. Unable to dislodge the creature from the boat's propellers, the captain returned to port and the sunfish was disentangled. Measuring 2½ feet thick and more than 10 feet long, the sunfish weighed a startling 4,400 pounds.

Seven-year-old Champion Rankin holds the 29-pound, 12-ounce king salmon he caught on Père Marquette Lake in Michigan.

Courtesy Dick Rankin

sured 40 inches from nose to tail and weighed 29 pounds, 12 ounces.

"My biggest salmon is on the wall of my shop," Rankin's father said. "That fish weighed 30 pounds even. I think if we had weighed Champion's fish right away, it would have come in at least at that much and maybe more."

Both Rankins are proud of their catch—especially Champion, who credits his father for all his angling success. "I can't thank my dad enough for getting me that big salmon," he said. "I hope next year he can find me another one."

SNAGGED BY THE EYELET

El Padre, as they called him, sat aboard the Mexican sportfisher *Indo Mable*, tugging on the first striped marlin of the day. His friend and fishing partner, Bob Nunn, stood on the deck and watched.

While El Padre dueled the marlin, the deckhand Roberto spotted a second striped marlin finning at the surface. He scrambled to the bait tank, removed a fresh *caballito,* impaled it through the eyes and flung it over the gunwale. The marlin gulped the bait and disappeared into the depths.

Roberto set the hook and handed the rod to Nunn, who had never caught a marlin. The rod, one that Nunn had borrowed from a friend, was custom-made with fancy, gold-colored rollers and an expensive big-game reel.

Suddenly, and much to Nunn's surprise, the marlin surged forward, yanking the rod from his grip. The borrowed rod and reel went flying over the railing and into the vast Sea of Cortez. Nunn was heartbroken. His very first marlin had not only escaped but taken his friend's expensive rod and reel with him.

Just then, Roberto spotted a third marlin near the boat. He selected another rod, baited the hook and immediately hooked the marlin. Warily, he handed the rod to Nunn, who was determined not to lose another fish—or another rod.

Nunn had fought the fish for 20 minutes when a rod with gold-colored rollers emerged from the water—the same rod and reel that had gone overboard! The rod had been snagged by its final tiny eyelet. Somehow Nunn's second marlin had crossed the path of his first and collided with the sinking rod and reel. The collision must have knocked the third marlin from the hook, which miraculously caught the eyelet.

Elated, Roberto reached over the transom and retrieved the custom rod. He removed the hook from the eyelet and handed the dripping rod to Nunn, who happily began to reel. The line was slack at first, but after a few spins on the reel it surged upward and a marlin jumped—the same marlin that had yanked the rod overboard!

By now, El Padre had released his fish and stood watching in amazement as Nunn brought the striped marlin alongside the boat. Roberto hurried to the railing and held the marlin by the bill. He removed the hook, released the fish and stepped back.

"El Padre Grande!" he shouted to the heavens, completing a swift Hail Mary and a bow to El Padre.

Father Ed Galyon, minister of the First Methodist Church in Camarillo, California, smiled. He was the one the locals called El Padre, and it was he who was credited with the miracle catch.

SEVEN-MINUTE GRANDER

Capt. Bobby Brown stood at the helm of the local charter boat *Kona Safari* in the waters off the coast of Kona, Hawaii.

The green slopes of the Mauna Hualalai volcano towered in the background. The island of Maui rose on the horizon. The boat's twin engines churned the surface of the sea, pulling the lures through their wake. All eyes aboard scanned the water, searching for something, anything, to indicate game fish.

Suddenly the shrill of a strike split the air. A crew member removed the rod from its holder and handed it to the angler. Brown shoved the throttles forward. Black exhaust swirled aft as a huge blue marlin broke the surface. Its head shook from side to side as it cleared the water and crashed back to the sea.

The fish leaped again, and again and again. Brown had seen many marlin, seen them jump and tailwalk and greyhound—but nothing to equal this.

"It was almost frightening," Brown said. "From the moment she was hooked, she never slowed. She just jumped back and forth across our stern."

For seven continual minutes, the marlin leaped. Awed by its power, the angler did what he could, keeping the line taut and waiting for the deep run to begin. But the fish never sounded. Only once did it break the jumping pattern by leaping toward the boat and forcing Brown to gun the engines forward.

"She never took more than a couple of hundred yards of line out," Brown said. "She just greyhounded across the water parallel with us, turned, and greyhounded back. We were ready, but we never had to chase her."

The lure was lodged deep in the fish's gullet, and seven minutes after hook-up, after one of the most remarkable aerial displays ever witnessed, the marlin had jumped itself to death.

The amazed crew boated the fish, which later weighed 1,170 pounds. The marlin was caught on 80-pound line and, but for the crewman handling the rod, would have set a new world record.

DID YOU KNOW?

Oxygen is more plentiful at the water's surface than below. Fast swimmers like the marlin and tuna need more oxygen and spend much of their lives near the surface. Slow swimmers like the grouper need less oxygen and remain near the bottom.

40 OUT OF 40— THE FINAL TROUT

Bob Smith reached down into the bottom of the rubber dinghy, scrounging for his pack of essentials. He found his pouch of tobacco and slowly filled his corncob pipe, watching as the breeze began to blow through the narrow canyon in the Sawtooth Mountains. His weathered hands cupped the flame. The taste of sweet tobacco filled his lungs. The lake's surface trembled with the wind that would soon screech down the cliffs as it had almost every day since Smith's arrival.

By the age of 80, Smith had caught and released all but one species of North American wild trout—the elusive Sunapee. For 20 years he had searched America's remote lakes and streams to fulfill his dream.

It had been three days since the guide and his string of pack mules bid Smith farewell, promising to return 10 days later. No sooner had the guide left than freezing rain began to fall, turning the ground to hard icy snow.

Alone, Smith had set camp in the cold. He chose a campsite near the lake, tucked in a copse surrounded by patches of dying timber. And for three days he waited. The sky remained clouded, the ground frozen. It was October, a cold and unpredictable time of year in the Idaho mountains.

Smith's small rubber dinghy rested outside the tent. Fishing gear leaned against the inside flap near

Courtesy Bob Smith

On his 81st birthday, Bob Smith trolls for what he hopes will be a dream come true—catching the last of the known North American wild trout species.

a tackle box and bedroll. A Coleman lantern buzzed within. A cot lay by the light. Smith tied flies and rested, waiting for his chance to fish. Outside, the wind howled through the trees, flinging sheets of snow across the secluded valley.

Finally, on the third day, the wind quieted and the clouds parted. It was Smith's 81st birthday, a bitter-cold day with a foot of snow clinging to the frozen ground. Eager to fish, Smith hurried to the lake's edge. The dinghy rowed easily. He trolled weighted flies all day, hoping for the strike that did not come.

The next morning he woke early and began working one of the few shoals near the far end of the lake. He was trolling a "Black Leech" fly along a sunken ridge when, without warning, the thin rod sprang forward. He hesitated, then snapped it back

and set the hook. The fish was much stronger than the familiar brook trout and made repeated runs without breaking water.

After a few minutes, Smith dipped his net into the water and saw his fish—a bright, silvery female Sunapee. She was 16 inches long and weighed nearly two pounds. Smith rowed to shore carrying his prized catch. He laid her on the frozen ground, recorded a few photographs and released her into the lake.

Standing at the bank, he watched as she swam away through the shallows. Tears welled in his eyes. Here, among the glittering peaks of the Sawtooth range, his quest had come to an end. He looked out across the lake and recalled each trout, each adventure, each body of water. At last, his dream was fulfilled.

Courtesy Bob Smith

Bob Smith's 40th out of 40 known North American wild trout: a female Sunapee that took him a lifetime to catch.

TANDEM MARLIN

"Reel 'em up!" Capt. Kenny Dickerson barked from the helm of the 48-foot sportfisher *Highland Queen*. "Swede, grab a couple of psychedelics. We need something to excite these fish."

Dickerson and his deckhand Swede were trolling the 209 bank near San Diego, California. It was the summer of 1964. The hippies were hip, everything was cool, and marlin jigs were "psychedelics": three colorful plastic feathers tied in a bunch, a crude lure that allowed boats to troll faster and cover more ground.

Dickerson glanced back at the lures and spotted two familiar tails bobbing in the wake. A sudden swipe of a bill and the starboard reel announced the first strike. The second marlin lagged behind, then jumped the line of its hooked companion and charged the portside lure. But there was no strike, and Swede reeled in the line

The guest that day was a novice angler from Michigan. His marlin strained against the line and was swimming parallel with the boat when Swede yelled for Dickerson to kill the engines. Swede ran along the gunwale, stopping halfway. He leaned over the water and moments later brought up a dead marlin.

"Where the hell did that come from?" Dickerson asked.

"Snagged in our line," Swede said. He untangled the line from the fish's tail—and just in time. The line shot off through the water, nearly jerking the angler overboard. Swede returned to his side, and the marlin was soon boated.

Both fish were striped marlin, and each one weighed approximately 120 pounds. Dickerson, who has since skippered for more than 30 years, is still impressed by the catch. "I've heard of two fish caught on the same line before," he said, "but they were fish that school in large numbers. These were the only two fish in the area. Not only that, but the second marlin wasn't even tail-wrapped. The line had cut into his tail at an angle and wedged into one of the vertebrae. We were lucky the line didn't break, or worse, cut off the fish's tail."

Courtesy the Grimaldi family

Gina Grimaldi *(left) and her twin sister Toni caught twin marlins in Bermuda on only their second deep-sea fishing trip.*

GIANT CATFISH CHOKEHOLD

Only one thing concerns John Pidcock when he fishes. Catfish. Large catfish. Catfish that lurk in dark, dangerous crevices. Catfish the size of pickle barrels.

Pidcock scouts the rivers of central Oklahoma for beaver dens, overhanging banks, large boulders and deep water holes—the probable places where catfish nest and spawn. He carries no fishing gear, just a ski rope for a stringer. He noodles. He swims into a murky catfish hole, gropes about for the smooth, motionless fish and attempts to provoke it to bite him. When the catfish attacks, Pidcock reaches into the fish's open mouth and pulls it out by hand. This practice, called noodling, is legal—and popular—in many southern states.

"We start in the spring," Pidcock explained, "just as soon as the water warms enough so a man can get in."

Noodling is not without risks, and Pidcock understands them well. Beaver bites, poisonous snakes, jagged rocks, and catfish so large some can hold a man down. "There was an old man who noodled over in Chicken Creek near Ten Killer Lake," Pidcock said. "He caught several fish 90 pounds and bigger back in the 1920s. One of those big flatheads bit him up past his elbow and raked all the meat off his forearm. They had to amputate his arm."

Courtesy John Pidcock

Noodler John Pidcock with the 48-pound flathead catfish he wrestled from a beaver den on the Deep Fork River near Luther, Oklahoma.

Pidcock retains his limbs, but two seasons ago, while feeling for a large catfish in a deserted beaver den on Cimmaron River, he was bitten on the hand by a startled muskrat. Pidcock, who plays guitar at a local club and noodles with gloves to protect his hands, had reached into the air pocket where the muskrat lived. The muskrat clamped its jaws around his fingers, sending a sudden numbing sensation down his hand.

> **❝That catfish weighed 48 pounds and its bottom jaw was as big around as a piece of luggage. When it clamped down on my hand, it bit so hard it broke one of my fingers.❞**

Pidcock returned to the river's edge and removed the bloodied glove. The top of the glove had been pierced, but there were no holes in the bottom. One of his fingers, however, had been bitten clean through. "The bottom teeth must have missed," Pidcock said, "but the top teeth went all the way through, just missing the bone."

In July of 1993, in the Deep Fork River, Pidcock noodled his largest catfish. He had squirmed far back into a beaver's den and cornered the fish. When it bit him, he reached into its mouth with both hands and grasped it by its thick, toothy lower lip.

Two of Pidcock's friends, Carl Harris and Ivan Church, stood at the entrance to the den and held his legs. Pidcock signaled, and his friends yanked him from the hole. The catfish emerged last, clamped to Pidcock's hands.

"That catfish weighed 48 pounds," Pidcock said, "and its bottom jaw was as big around as a piece of luggage. When it clamped down on my hand, it bit so hard it broke one of my fingers."

Noodlers target catfish during spawning season, when the usually docile fish become aggressive and are enticed to bite. They look forward all winter to the day they can shimmy through the small basketball-size tunnels that lead from the riverbank into large underground beaver dens where the large catfish lie, waiting to spawn and quick to attack.

"There's nothing more gratifying than getting bit by a big catfish," Pidcock said. "The adrenaline rush is unbelievable."

75 MARLIN IN ONE DAY

Capt. Mike "Beak" Hurt has caught a lot of fish during his 20-odd years at the helm. But when he and his crew arrived in Cabo San Lucas, Mexico, after a three-day haul from San Diego, "a lot of fish" took on a whole new meaning.

"I was skippering a 46-foot Hatteras for a client who was to come in by plane the next day," Hurt said. "We had a free day to fish, so we called up a few other boats and went out to fan the area. John 'Zuker' Lloyd, who was on the *Galaxy*, had gone to the Jaime Banks and was first to report fish. By the time he radioed their third strike, we were on our way."

Hurt and his crew had reached the edge of the Jaime Banks when their first marlin hit. It was a striper and was soon caught and released. The lines were quickly reset when three more marlin rushed the lures. One jumped off, and the other two were caught.

The action never slowed. There were single, double and multiple hook-ups. The marlin were so abundant that hookless lures were trolled as teasers and baits were cast to the finning fish. Baits were drifted and trolled and lowered with weights. Every fishing technique the crew tried worked. "It was remarkable," Hurt said. "We couldn't stay away from the schooling marlin long enough to catch fresh bait."

The climax of the day came while the fishermen drifted above a meatball of mackerel. The anglers were free-spooling live bait over the meatball when suddenly all eight of them hooked up. As the eight lines raced to the surface, the anglers scrambled to keep them from tangling.

"That was a first for me," Hurt said, "probably a first anywhere in the world. The marlin were like missiles coming up all around us. Everybody was scrambling. All I could do was watch."

Two of the marlin threw the hook, but the remaining six of the "double-quadruple strike" were caught and released. And the marlin kept coming. By the end of the day the count was 75.

"It was an unbelievable day," Hurt said. "The poor guys never got a break."

DID YOU KNOW?

A 10-pound bluefin tuna tagged and released in 1974 weighed 605 pounds when caught 12 years later.

A Criminal Catch, and Casting for Deer

Strange things have happened to Bob Thiry while fishing. During a walleye outing, he snagged a parcel of money from a lake and helped convict a criminal. A few weeks later, while pike fishing on a river, he hooked a wayward doe . . .

Thiry had fished Cross Lake for nearly 30 years. Located in Pine City, Minnesota, the six-mile-long lake brims with fish. Bass, walleye and Thiry's favorite species, the northern pike, all inhabit the lake.

Wearing waders, Thiry stood in a few feet of water and cast his lure.

"I hadn't been on that particular side of the lake for at least four or five years," Thiry said, "and that morning I had this feeling to go back over there and fish for northerns and walleyes." He began to wind the reel when something struck the lure. "I gave the line a jerk, and the way it reacted, I thought I'd hooked a big snapping turtle."

Thiry pulled again, and a shiny brass handle emerged from the water. He reeled the object to the shore, leaned down and removed a satchel from the hook. It was filled with bundles of uncanceled checks and a stack of "Accounts Receivable" ledger sheets from the local feed mill. Thiry looked at the first check and recognized the name. The ledger sheet had familiar names on it also, and with account balances in the thousands of dollars.

Thiry was astounded. "There was no cash, but the checks totaled more than $13,000 and the ledger sheets were worth many times more than that to the mill's owner."

Having spent most of his life in the small town of Pine City, Thiry knew everyone personally—including the owner of the feed mill. "It was very early in the morning when I caught the satchel," he said, "so I went into the town and stopped at the bakery for a cup of coffee and bumped into the sheriff. I'd been out of town for a few weeks, so I asked him if there had been any recent robberies. He told me there had been two the other night, and one of the robberies was at the Pine City Mill. I told him, 'You won't believe this, but I just fished their cotton-pickin' satchel out of the lake!'"

With permission from the sheriff, Thiry took the satchel directly to the mill's owner. He walked into his friend's office and asked him if he was having trouble with the law. The puzzled owner stared at him in confusion. Thiry smiled, placed the satchel on the desk and asked his friend why he would have thrown all of his records into the lake.

"My buddy couldn't believe it," Thiry said. "He was so happy, he nearly went berserk. That was the only ledger he had of all his charge accounts. The find saved him a bundle of money."

The next day, the owner of the mill delivered four quarts of Canadian Club whiskey to Thiry's home. The sheriff was also grateful. The recovered satchel and Thiry's testimony helped convict the robber, who was captured while attempting to cross the Minnesota border into Canada.

Three uneventful weeks went by. Thiry and a friend were fishing for pike in Minnesota's Snake River. Drifting quietly in a boat along the river, the two men cast floating plugs toward shore. Thiry pitched his lure across the water, gently thumbing the open-faced reel. The lure splashed on the surface, but before he could stop the free-spinning reel, a bird's nest of fishing line backlashed around the spool.

"It was a mess," Thiry said. "I was trying to untangle the line when I heard a splash and saw a whitetail doe swimming across the river. She was heading right for my line, and all I could do was hope she'd swim over it."

Working frantically, Thiry had just managed to free the final knot on the spool when the deer swam into his line. The lure caught in her brisket and almost yanked the rod from Thiry's grip.

"I held my fishing rod for dear life," he said. "I was fishing a strong line, 35-pound test, and I didn't want to lose the whole setup. Luckily, just as the deer sprinted off for the woods, the line broke."

Thiry, who is well known in Pine City for his white-tail deer hunting skills, was dumfounded.

"We were drifting so quietly," he said, "that the deer never saw us. She got across the river all right, but she took my pike plug with her."

DOUBLE SUPER GRAND SLAM

"The fishing that year had been phenomenal," Capt. Tim Choate said. "I was working as a crew member in LaGuaira, Venezuela, on a 48-foot Jim Smith-built sportfisher named *Escapade*. It was early fall, 1984, and we had just caught our thousandth billfish of the year. We had also captured seven Grand Slams, and we took the high-point award in the International Women's Fishing Association's 1984 tournament."

"Grand Slam" is the term used when a blue marlin, a white marlin and a sailfish are caught in one day. A "Double" Grand Slam is the successful landing of two of each of these billfish species in one day. And a "Super" Grand Slam is when, on the same day, an angler on the boat catches a swordfish.

"The anticipation was incredible the day after we caught our seventh Grand Slam," Choate said. "We had the same guests on board: world-class anglers Bob Herder, Bud German and Terry Detrich. They caught more than a dozen billfish as part of the Grand Slam the day before, and our enthusiasm was high."

The LaGuaira skies were clear and its seas calm. Choate prepared the fresh ballyhoo baits as the captain navigated full speed to the local blue marlin hole. Lines were set at 9:15 in the morning, and 30 minutes later a small blue marlin was caught, tagged and released.

"Moments after we released the small blue," Choate said, "two reels went off and two sailfish jumped beyond our stern. We caught one of the sailfish and lost the other when it ate everything but the bait's head off the hook."

Thirty more minutes passed. Another sailfish took a bait and was quickly caught and released. The fishing lines were retrieved and the baits were replaced with lures. The captain increased the trolling speed and drove toward a new location.

"On our way to the new grounds," Choate said, "Bob Herder rigged a special homemade lure and soon, after putting it out, we hooked our second blue marlin. It was a larger fish and after an hour-and-a-half battle, the blue marlin was gaffed and boated for a mount."

The next few hours were slow, and by early afternoon the captain altered course and drove the boat to the local white marlin location. By 2:45 in the afternoon the group had their first white marlin and the boat's eighth Grand Slam of the year.

"There was a lot of daylight left," Choate said, "so we continued to fish. By 5:15 we had another sailfish. Moments later we hooked and released a white marlin that inhaled two baits without slowing down. And eight minutes later Bud German caught another white marlin, more than enough for a Double Grand Slam!"

The anglers continued to fish and by nightfall had added three more white marlin to the count. It had been a remarkable day. As the lines were retrieved for the final time, the captain issued orders to prepare for swordfishing.

"We derigged the 20-pound outfits," Choate said, "and rerigged them with 80-pound gear. The captain soon located a likely-looking section of the 200-fathom ledge and throttled back to neutral. By 7:15 we had three baits in the water."

The night sea was calm when the ratchet of a fishing reel slowly clicked with a swordfish strike. As Detrich worked the rod, a second reel sounded a strike. Herder grabbed it, and soon both fish were hooked solidly.

"Bob Herder's fish was no match for the 80-pound outfit," Choate said, "and we quickly had the first swordfish of the night. It was a Super Grand Slam and we were still hooked to another fish."

Detrich kept the reel's drag loose and patiently played his fish. The fish had stripped most of the fishing line from the spool and fought stubbornly from the deep water.

"We weren't positive it was a swordfish," Choate said, "so Terry was being careful just in case. Finally the fish came up, and I was able to take a first wrap on the leader. Then the fish broke surface, and I yelled, 'It's a swordfish! It's a swordfish!' It was larger than the first one, and Tom successfully gaffed it and brought it aboard. All of us started yelling. It was the first Double Super Grand Slam we'd ever heard of."

The elated fishermen returned to the dock and celebrated their once-in-a-lifetime catch. It was a remarkable fishing accomplishment.

Courtesy Bob Herder

A sampling of the only known Double Super Grand Slam. From left to right: Tom Ross, Tim Choate and Mike Aman.

SHARK-FRIENDLY

On a warm April morning Mike Leech, head of the International Game Fish Association, his wife and his father set out in Leech's 36-foot fishing boat, *Off Call*, into the gulf stream for a few days of fishing.

"It was Saturday," Leech said, "and we trolled south from the north side of Bimini and caught a few dolphinfish, barracudas and one amberjack that we tagged and released. At noon we anchored in about 30 feet of water in the lee of some little rock islands just north of Cat Cay. My wife, Gussie, fixed up sandwiches, and I dropped over a bag of chum and rigged up some light lines for bottom fishing."

The fishing was good, and soon the Leeches' live well was filled with small groupers and yellowtail snappers. The three anglers finished lunch, pulled-up anchor and went to troll the edge of the gulf stream.

Leech took three lively yellowtails from the live well and rigged them for trolling. He placed two baits on the outriggers and sent the third bait down 100 feet on a downrigger. Gussie captained the boat. Leech and his dad waited for the strike. Less than an hour had passed when a dusky shark appeared on the surface. It followed the boat, descended and attacked the deep bait.

"My dad took the rod," Leech said, "and after a 10-minute fight he had the six-and-a-half-foot shark beside the boat. I tagged the shark with a bright yellow tag from the National Marine Fisheries Service and cut it loose. As I cut the leader, I also cut a plastic strap that had become tangled around the shark and was slicing into its body."

Leech rerigged three fresh baits, and five minutes later both outriggers bounced with a strike. Leech and his father grabbed the bent rods and soon realized they were fighting the same fish. It was a shark, and hanging from its back was a bright yellow tag.

"It was the same shark," Leech said, "and it had swallowed both our baits. I cut both leaders and watched again as the shark swam away. I put out three fresh yellowtail baits, and Gussie maneuvered the boat ahead slowly."

Five more minutes had passed when both outriggers again bounced with a double strike. Leech and his dad set the hooks and anxiously awaited the leap of a large fish. Instead they glimpsed a shark and their familiar bright yellow tag.

"We got the shark in," Leech said, "and I cut the leaders from the fourth and fifth hook in this shark's jaw. We were getting low on bait, so I told Gussie to put the boat up to cruising speed and leave the area."

Gussie steered the boat north and with the current. She drove a mile and a half at full speed before slowing the boat to begin the troll. Leech set out three lively yellowtails and waited. Thirty minutes had passed when the rod tip of the deep bait arched from the weight of a large fish. Leech's dad held the rod and pulled. Minutes later, a dusky shark with a bright yellow tag emerged from the depths.

"We couldn't believe it," Leech said. "It was our same shark with our same yellow tag hanging from its back. It was the sixth time in less than an hour that I had cut a leader on this shark."

Leech rigged a batch of dead mullet, and Gussie turned the boat toward home. The live yellowtails were gone and the shark never returned.

Another shark story: this blue marlin probably never knew what hit him. Bob Jones (right) and his daughter Alicia were fighting the blue marlin 15 miles from Tortola Island in the British Virgin Islands when the line suddenly went slack. The estimated 3,000-pound shark had severed the 600-pound marlin in one vicious bite.

Courtesy Bob Jones

THROW OUT THE CATFISH WITH THE BATH WATER

66I knew nobody would believe my story if I didn't have the fish. So I took it all the way back to Tucson and put it in my bathtub.99

Mel Coulston and his one-year-old son, Mel Jr., sat on the bank of Piña Blanca Lake 45 miles south of Tucson, Arizona, near the Mexican border. Coulston fished catfish while his son bounced blissfully in a baby-bouncer at the edge of the lake.

It was midday, and the fishing had been good. Coulston rigged a chunk of bloody chicken livers and flung it into the lake. Less than an hour had passed when a wandering catfish sniffed the rank hors d'oeuvre.

"I got a hook-up with a good-size cat," Coulston said. "Probably a nine-pounder. As I was fighting it, my son started moving up and down in his bouncer. He bounced himself right into the lake. When he hit the water,

he turned on his back and started to sink. Luckily, he was wearing a jumper, which helped slow his descent."

The edge of the lake plunged sharply to a depth of seven to eight feet. Coulston leaped into the water, dropping his fishing rod in midflight, reached down, clutched his sinking son from the water and scrambled up the steep bank. The bouncer chair was perched at the water's edge. The rod and reel were gone.

Coulston returned to his car, and both father and son changed into dry clothes. Coulston unpacked a spare rod and reel and returned with his child to the location of their mishap. Coulston pierced another chicken liver and slung it into the deep water.

"I didn't get a bite for a while," Coulston said, "so I started to reel in my line. It got heavy, but not with a fish. I kept reeling, and out of the water came my other fishing pole. I couldn't believe my luck. I took the pole off the hook and felt a strong tug at the end of the line. It was the fish I'd caught earlier, and it was still hooked!"

Coulston landed the catfish and excitedly dropped it into a large styrofoam cooler. He filled the cooler with water and ice, and with help from another fisherman carried it and the baby to his car.

"I knew nobody would believe my story if I didn't have the fish," Coulston said. "So I took it with me all the way back to Tucson and put it in my bathtub."

The large catfish nearly filled the length of the tub. Coulston invited friends to witness the entombed catch. The next morning, he placed the catfish in the cooler and returned to Piña Blanca Lake.

"It's about an hour's drive each way," Coulston said, "but the catfish didn't seem to mind. The ice kept the water cold like the lake. I never intended to kill the catfish, just show him off some. When I got to the lake, I carried him back to where I caught him and let him go free. He swam off like nothing had ever happened."

REDEEMED

Chris Muhleman spent a summer in the seaside village of Garibaldi, Oregon, working as a deckhand aboard the charter boat *D&D 1*. The boat was docked in Tillamook Bay, nestled along the rugged shores of the western coast of Oregon.

"It was a fun summer," Muhleman remembered, "getting paid to help people catch fish. The captain patiently taught me the finer points of salmon fishing from sunup to sundown, and my angling skills improved as each day passed."

Muhleman fished whenever he had the opportunity, usually during lulls in the daily charters. He used the heavy-tackle rental gear stored aboard the boat, and by late July he longed for the challenge of catching a large salmon on light tackle. "Less than two weeks remained in the fishing season," he said. "So I went to the local bank, withdrew my savings and walked across the street to the local tackle store. I had saved all summer to buy a $150 graphite rod

Chris Muhleman, shown here with a good-size silver salmon.

Courtesy Chris Muhleman

and a premium spinning reel, and now I finally had enough money to do it."

The next day, the weather was ideal for fishing. The early-morning air was cool and not a breeze of wind brushed the bay. Six excited passengers climbed aboard the 28-foot boat, anxious to start the day. After the usual introductions, Muhleman unfastened the dock ropes, refilled the coffee cups, and prepared the deck as the captain drove the boat to the fishing grounds.

Outside the bay, the sea heaved and dipped in large, glossy swells. The captain turned north along the coast to an area off Nehalem Bay where large silver salmon were rumored to be feeding.

"The skipper slowed near a promising rip," Muhleman said, "and I quickly prepared all the fishing gear. Soon the anglers were happily fishing, waiting for their lines to go taut. I fetched my shiny new outfit, baited the hook with herring and tossed the line into the swirling water. The boat only had six rod holders, one for each passenger, so I wedged the rod butt of my fishing pole into a scupper hole. It seemed secure, and I was close enough to grab it if a large fish tried to yank it loose."

Fifteen minutes passed without a strike. Muhleman had just turned to get a soda when a large salmon struck his line forcefully and flipped the graphite rod from the scupper and into the water.

"I was devastated," Muhleman said. "It all happened so fast, I never had a chance. Then suddenly a hooked salmon came to the surface, thrashing its head and trying to throw the hook. I could see my rod under the water and trailing behind the fish, so I yelled to the anglers to reel in their lines. The skipper turned the boat and gunned the engines toward the fish, and I got a net and crawled out to the bow."

Muhleman knelt on the bow and tried to scoop the fish into the net, but each time it was just beyond his reach. The captain carefully paralleled the salmon. Other charter boats drifted nearby, and their captains cheered and jeered Muhleman's antics from their helms.

"The whole fleet was having a great time watching me stab away futilely from the bow," Muhleman said. "I was heartbroken when the fish disappeared. I knew my good name would be tarnished forever. I sadly returned to the stern and rigged our passengers' fishing rods and baited all their hooks. I pulled in the heavy lead cable that we were using to keep the fishing lines at a constant depth. I had forgotten to do this earlier, so we had been dragging the cable behind the boat as we tried to net my fish. I pulled the cable out of the water and was snapping in the baited fishing lines when I saw my graphite rod. My rod and reel had gotten caught in the cable."

Excitedly, Muhleman reached down and removed the tangled rod from the cable. He was reeling the slack fishing line when it jerked and spun from the reel.

Startled by the unexpected jolt, Muhleman leaned back against the weight. "I was certain the fish had broken off," he said. "Now I had him on again. I held the fishing rod extra tight, and five minutes later I boated a 15-pound silver salmon.

"It was the biggest one of the season, and everyone called on the radio to congratulate me on the catch. It was a great feeling, especially since only minutes earlier I was sure I'd lost everything."

RELEASED TODAY, CAUGHT TOMORROW

The first few days of fishing had been productive for Tom and Polly Gillen, owners of *Pizazz*, a 38-foot Uniflite, captained by Cami Garnier. They were near Cabo San Lucas, Mexico, and had tagged and released three striped marlin and lost a fourth at the strike. Then a north wind began to blow, forcing them back to Cabo San Lucas, where they patiently waited out the five-day storm.

On the sixth day, the weather cleared. Garnier started up the engines and the three headed for the Gorda Banks—a reef 24 miles northeast of Cabo San Lucas. They soon found action and had begun to work a school of dorado when Garnier spotted a striped marlin tailing downswell. Tom took a 12-pound light tackle rig, pinned on live mackerel and ran to the bow. He flung the bait toward the marlin and waited.

It was a perfect cast. The marlin attacked the bait, and after a 45-minute fight Tom brought the fish alongside the gunwale. Garnier hurried down from the bridge and grabbed the leader when he noticed a tag dangling from the marlin's flank. He removed the old tag, sank a new one and released the fish unharmed.

Later that afternoon, as they returned to their mooring, Tom inspected the tag. The serial numbers on the shaft looked familiar. He scrounged through their stack of tagging cards and to his wonderment discovered the tag was theirs. It was the same tag they had used six days earlier!

The marlin, showing no signs of the previous battle, had moved from the tip of Baja 24 miles north into the Sea of Cortez. The repeat catch was a spectacular feat and a first in billfishing history.

Striped marlin abound in Cabo San Lucas waters.

Courtesy Connie Sue White

22 GOLDEN RECORDS

To get to the record-holding lakes of California's Sierra Nevada Mountains, Don Vachini and his sons hike hours and often days over jumbled talus, icy snow-fields and remote ridgelines. They hunt trout with fly gear, and since 1987 they've recorded 22 golden trout world records and 5 brook trout world records.

"We've been backpacking ever since Jason and Matt were 9 and 10 years old," Vachini said. "We would hike to specific lakes where we knew the golden trout lived. These fish fascinated us, and when the IGFA opened a fly record class for them we returned to the lakes to set records."

Golden trout are considered by many to be the most beautiful species of the trout family. Native only to California, they have been successfully transplanted to high-altitude lakes in Washington, Idaho and Wyoming. The All-Tackle World Record was caught in Cook's Lake, Wyoming, and weighed 11 pounds.

To catch the record fish, the Vachinis trekked above the timberline, sometimes as high as 12,000 feet above sea level, timing their arrival with the lake's first thaw. Only during this period, known as "ice-out," are the golden trout readily accessible from the shoreline.

"The lakes up there are often 50 to 60 acres wide," Vachini said, "too big to randomly cast your fly. At ice-out the fish move into the inlets and will be stacked in large schools numbering 15 to 20 fish, each fish weighing from one to four pounds."

The high-altitude lakes are sunk into bare granite craters with no surrounding cover to conceal a fisherman. Golden trout swim apprehensively along the shoreline and once spooked may not return for days. When he finds a fish-filled inlet, Vachini must slink ahead low, slowly inching along the granite bank on his belly. He carries a fly rod in one hand and pulls himself along the harsh rock with the other.

"I wear knee pads when I crawl along the granite," Vachini said, "and when I get to the water I lie down flat on my back and lean up just a little to cast in a semi-prone position. It's not very comfortable, but it's the only way to get close to the fish. I've lost a lot of fishing

DID YOU KNOW?

The most venomous fish in the world is the stonefish. Found in the Indo-Pacific region, the stonefish has spines that contain deadly poison. Without anti-venom, agonizing death usually occurs within six hours.

days by being careless, but now, moving slowly, I can get right next to the fish."

While fishing, Vachini strips the fly line onto the top of his stomach and often watches the fish take the fly. The casting is exhausting, and he trains all year to keep his stomach fit. "During one stop," he said, "I could have set four IGFA fly records, but I got such bad abdominal and back pains that I had to stop fishing."

Of the fishing family's 27 world records, 5 are recognized by the IGFA and 22 by the National Freshwater Fishing Hall of Fame.

"A one-pound golden trout in California is considered a trophy fish," Vachini said. "But the guys in Wyoming keep beating our records. That's where the really big fish are, so next year we may go to Wyoming to try and take back some of our records."

The Vachinis have 27 more than most anglers. Odds are, they'll get to 28 soon.

One of Don Vachini's many world record golden trouts. This IGFA 20-pound tippet-class record fish weighed 1 pound even. The record was beaten in 1992 by an angler fishing Thumb Lake, Wyoming.

Courtesy Don Vachini

THE DIME AND THE DOLPHINFISH

Tony Pittman and his son Scott were marveling at the clarity of Key West's turquoise sea. Reaching into his pocket, Scott pulled out a shiny new dime and held it out for his father to see.

"How far down do you think we can watch it sink?" he asked.

"No more than 800 feet," Capt. Ken Harris quipped. "Because that's when it'll hit bottom."

Harris was owner and skipper of the fishing boat *Finesse*, which Tony Pittman had chartered for the day. He was accustomed to his clients' fascination with Florida's clear water and had seen many dimes go over the side.

Scott flicked the dime overboard and watched it flutter slowly down through the water, glittering as sunlight struck it. Harris finished tying a knot and glanced over the gunwale.

"That's bright enough to be a lure," he said, joking with the clients from Pennsylvania. "Watch a dolphinfish swim by and take it."

Just then a school of shadows darted by. The dime was forgotten and freshly rigged baits were thrown over. It was a school of dolphinfish, and after catching four or five dinner-size fish Harris moved the boat elsewhere in search of larger game.

Later that day, when they arrived at the docks, Scott grabbed a fillet knife and began to clean their catch. He sliced open the belly of the first dolphinfish and emptied the contents.

"Hey, you're never gonna believe this!" he hollered, looking down at the table.

There, among the half-digested squid and red crabs, was the shiny new dime that Scott had tossed into the water earlier in the day.

DID YOU KNOW?

Seven pairs of stockings, 47 buttons, 3 leather belts and 9 shoes were found inside the belly of a shark caught in the Philippine Islands. Another shark, caught in the Adriatic, had a raincoat, 3 overcoats and a car's license plate in its stomach. And a shark measuring 22 feet, caught in the Mediterranean Sea, had in its belly the headless body of a man wearing a full suit of armor.

FREE-GAFFING
A GIANT YELLOWFIN

Capt. Ted Dunn, owner and operator of the 92-foot *Royal Star* charter boat, hurried along the slippery deck, assisting his anglers and crew. It was two in the morning, and they were fishing for tuna near Socorro Island, Mexico, 500 miles south of Cabo San Lucas.

The bright lights of the *Royal Star* shone deep into the water, illuminating schools of frenzied yellowfin tuna. Baits splashed on the surface, reels sang out, and occasional thuds against the hull of the boat signaled another kamikaze tuna.

"Sometimes when tuna are hooked," Dunn explained, "the lights confuse them and they turn back toward you. It's a hell of a bang when a 200-pound tuna hits your boat."

The yellowfin stayed nearby, teased by the chum man's supply of anchovies. Finally a short lull in the action gave Dunn his first break of the night. He was standing at the gunwale, staring into the water, when a large tuna appeared alongside the boat.

Unable to resist the challenge, Dunn grabbed a gaff and leaned over the gunwale. As another large yellowfin swam by, he lunged down with the gaff. The snagged fish thrashed violently to escape. Dunn struggled to hold the bucking gaff. Two crew members sank two more gaffs into the fish and lifted it aboard, still alive and fighting furiously.

"The tuna went crazy when we brought him over the side," Dunn said. "We had to work fast. A hot fish will destroy everything that gets in his way."

The fish was subdued, stowed in the freezer and, upon their arrival 10 days later in San Diego, raised to the scales. The uncommon catch weighed an impressive 186 pounds!

Courtesy Capt. Ted Dunn

Capt. Ted Dunn with the 186-pound yellowfin tuna he free-gaffed while fishing at Socorro Island, Mexico.

SNAGGED BY THE SWIVEL

Willard Stanfield and his angling pal, Lewis R. Bennington, fished from the bank of the Nisqually River south of Tacoma, Washington. It was the winter of 1956 and the river flourished with fish. Stanfield molded the clump of roe around his fishhook and tied a strand of red yarn to the eyelet for color. He cast the bait into the river and let it sink to the bottom. The current was swift and cold, chilled by the melting snow of nearby Mt. Rainier.

"As the bait settled to the rocky bottom," Stanfield said, "I got a strike and set the hook. I started playing the fish, and after a few minutes he broke the water. As he jumped, I could see my yarn and bait about two feet in front of him. I didn't understand what was going on. The bait should have been in the fish's mouth. In fact, I shouldn't have been able to see the yarn at all."

Stanfield had no explanation for the aberration. The yarn was his, and the salmon that jumped was the only fish hooked in the vicinity. Baffled, Stanfield played the salmon, and after a brief but strenuous battle brought the fish to the bank of the river.

"I couldn't believe what I saw," Stanfield said. "I had hooked the eyelet of a swivel that was attached to a two-foot leader that was hooked to the salmon. Somebody had lost the fish earlier, and somehow my hook had snagged the trailing swivel."

Stanfield unhooked the fish and placed it in the cooler, all the while marveling at the accomplishment. He removed his hook from the swivel and replayed the scene in his mind.

The 10-pound king salmon had been swimming upriver and against the powerful current when Stanfield's small hook snagged the moving swivel. The hook had been swaying in the flowing current a few inches above the rocks and a few feet from the small lead pencil-weight that bounced along the rocky bottom. For Stanfield's hook to have slipped into the minuscule opening of the traveling swivel was extraordinary.

"It was the most remarkable thing that's happened to me fishing," Stanfield said. "It had to be at least a one-in-a-million catch."

DID YOU KNOW?

In 1968, Walter Kummerow set a world record for freshwater casting. His throw, confirmed by the International Casting Federation, measured 574 feet, 2 inches—nearly the distance of two football fields.

ONE-ON-ONE WITH 815 POUNDS OF BLUE MARLIN

Capt. Freddy Rice was fishing alone from his 31-foot charter boat *Ihu Nui*. It was a day originally set aside for boat maintenance, but a last-minute cancellation by Rice's mechanic freed the day for fishing.

"I go out alone whenever I can," the tireless Rice said. "It lets me experiment with new equipment, riggings and strategies."

Rice quietly motored from the harbor, caught bait, and by midday was working the waters above the thousand-fathom ledge north of Kona, Hawaii.

"I was fishing two baits, a *kawakawa* (little tunny) on the short line, and an *aku* (skipjack) on the long one. It was about noon when a line snapped from the outrigger. I turned to set the hook and saw the fish on the surface, shaking her head. She was a big Pacific blue, and I knew by her actions that she had swallowed the bait completely."

Rice held the rod firmly in his sun-leathered hands and moved to the starboard side of the boat, where he could run the controls and fight the fish at the same time. For 20 minutes he backed the boat down on the fish, keeping the line taut and away from the stern.

"When I had her within 120 feet, I increased the pressure and she jumped. It was my first clear view of her, and I estimated her weight at 700 pounds. I was ready with my tagging stick and camera when she suddenly took off across the surface. The battle intensified and the predator instinct in me took over. I decided to land this fish . . . if I could."

Rice set the reel's drag to its limit and for the next two hours battled alone across 10 miles of sea. The double line was up eight times during the final 20 minutes, only to disappear each time.

DID YOU KNOW?

A black marlin tagged and released in 1983 off Cabo San Lucas, Mexico, was recaptured 20 months later by a Japanese longliner near Norfolk Island, 5,763 miles away. The record-setting marlin had reached the island, about 400 miles north of New Zealand, by averaging 9.4 nautical miles per day.

A pleased Capt. Freddy Rice aboard his charter boat, Ihu Nui, after single-handedly landing this 815-pound blue marlin.

Courtesy Capt. Freddy Rice

Rice's arms and hands were numb. He knew he couldn't last another deep descent by the marlin. And then the battle was over. The marlin made one final jump and rolled to her side.

"The end of the fight was the most difficult. I put in the jaw hook and made two half hitches around the bill. But my energy was spent. My arms and hands seemed disconnected from my brain and wouldn't or couldn't function the way I wanted them to."

Later that afternoon, after cleating his catch to the transom of his boat, Rice arrived at Kona Harbor. The fish was hoisted onto the scales and weighed a staggering 815 pounds.

"This was one of the highlights of my career," Rice said. "Few things can match the challenge of fighting a big fish alone. I knew she could have dragged me into the rough inter-island channel and broken free, and that would only have been fair. I was lucky. This wasn't a matter of who was the strongest, but rather who first became the weakest."

TROUT FRENZY

Tourists travel from around the globe to experience the splendor of Yellowstone National Park. Most come to witness the animals roaming unobstructed by the thousands.

But fish, too, inhabit the park and proliferate wild and unfettered. Not many visitors know of the fishing and most never stray from the roadways. But some, like park ranger Michael Johns, eagerly search Yellowstone's lakes and back country at every opportunity for pristine streams and hidden shorelines.

In the summer of 1974, Johns and his wife pitched their tent in a clearing near a secluded bank on Yellowstone Lake. It was spawning season, and soon the many creeks and rivers would swell with libidinous trout.

Johns carried his fishing gear to the lake's edge near the mouth of a wide stream. He pitched a small lure into the water and began to reel. The water swirled as an 18-inch cutthroat trout pounced instantly.

"There were no signs of the fish on the surface," Johns said. "I chose the spot because it was near the mouth of the stream. I got a strike on every cast, even with my 4-pound test fishing line. I had hoped to bring lighter line, but 4-pound was the lightest I could find at the time. The trout didn't care. Ten out of 10 casts brought a fish. It was the most extraordinary fishing day of my life."

Johns carried a pair of hospital hemostats on his belt and released each trout quickly with the pliers-like instrument. "I was told by a fisheries biologist that this was the best way to release fish. He said that if I touched the fish, they would probably get a fungus and die. So the first thing I did was go to the local hospital and get some disposable hemostats. When I got to the lake, I cut two of the three hooks off my lure and pinched the barb down on the third."

Trout swarmed beneath the surface at the mouth of the stream, waiting to invade the shallow water and spawn. They were vivid and brightly colored and furiously fought the hook. All of Johns' trout were large and most were similar in size.

The action was relentless—so remarkable, in fact, that Johns kept a count of every catch he made.

"I fished for two hours," Johns said, "and finally had to quit at 133 fish because my fingers hurt so bad from twisting the hook out of the fishes' mouths with the hemostats.

"The 63rd fish was the first trout I landed that was under 14 inches, and out of the 133 only two measured less than 14 inches. Most of the trout were 16 to 18 inches long. The biggest one measured 20 inches."

For two continuous hours, Johns had landed more than one trout a minute. It was an impressive accomplishment, even in Yellowstone's enchanted park.

SWORDFISH TUG-OF-WAR

Just the mention of swordfish is enough to incite passion in the hearts of fishermen. Famed for their unyielding strength and defiance of the hook, the broadbill has pushed many anglers to the brink of madness and reduced others to states of delirium.

But the years have not been kind to the swordfish. Their prized flanks bring a high price at market, and competition for these golden billfish is fierce.

Don and Millie Allison know firsthand just how fierce that can be.

They were in southern California in the early 1970s aboard *Hoaloha*, their 42-foot custom Hatteras. Two experienced anglers out for an enjoyable day of fishing, they had the good fortune of coming upon a large swordfish sunning its back in the waters off Santa Barbara Island. The broadbill, an old warrior missing the tip of its dorsal

fin, was slowly cruising south across the afternoon chop.

"Millie took the controls," Don recalled, "while I went down and rigged a fresh mackerel. She eased up close, and I dropped the bait into the water. Minutes later we had the hook-up."

The two anglers were prepared for the expected battle, and an hour and a half later the fish finally surfaced—a magnificent swordfish, big and strong and thick across the shoulders. Don cranked the reel evenly, working the rod with care. Millie patiently worked the boat, as she had so many times before.

66Don't hit that fish! He's on our line!99

The swordfish was less than two boat-lengths away when suddenly from abeam the boat came a large commercial vessel, full speed ahead, the plank off its bow bearing down on their catch. It was the *Santa Lucia*, a local commercial harpooning boat intent on the Allisons' swordfish.

"Don't hit that fish!" Millie screamed. "He's on our line!" But the man on the plank ignored her pleas, reared back and thrust a deadly harpoon into the hooked fish. Coils of thick yellow nylon rope and brightly colored floats followed.

"We've just stuck a rod-and-reel fish!" the captain of the *Santa Lucia* declared excitedly to a friend over the radio. "Whose is it?"

"Whoever has the heaviest gear," replied the friend.

Millie was irate. The swordfish had sounded, and while Don worked feverishly to retrieve it, she maneuvered the boat to keep their line away from the harpooner's coarse rope. Meanwhile, the *Santa Lucia* circled, waiting for the harpoon buoys to resurface.

Twenty more minutes passed before the wounded fish was again within gaffing range. Don seized the leader and gaffed the fish. He cut the harpooner's rope from the buoys and tied the fish to the stern. Millie turned and headed back to port.

Still circling nearby, the *Santa Lucia* called the Allisons on the radio.

"We got it in the head, didn't we?" they taunted.

The Allisons did not respond, and the *Santa Lucia* quickly faded from sight.

Many other boats had been tuned to the same radio frequency and had heard the confrontation. By the time the Allisons arrived back at the docks, the airwaves from San Diego to San Francisco were buzzing with the news. The swordfish was hoisted to the weigh-scale with the dart of the harpoon still lodged by its dorsal. The fish weighed 448 pounds—the largest catch of the year.

Elated by the catch, the Allisons did not file a complaint against the *Santa Lucia* or its crew. Their tarnished reputation, the result of all the publicity about the incident, would suffice.

The harpoon dart was saved, however, as a reminder of the year's most unusual catch.

165-Pound Tuna Lost and Found

In March 1981, Dr. Mas Itano and his wife Teri were two of 28 passengers aboard the *Royal Polaris*, a 113-foot charter fishing boat from Fisherman's Landing, San Diego, California. They were enjoying a 16-day trip to the Revillagigedo Islands, a cluster of small islands located off the southern tip of Baja California, Mexico.

On this particular night, the boat was anchored at Roca Partida, the smallest island of the chain. Itano was fishing for yellowfin tuna with live bait caught the day before at Uncle Sam Bank. But Itano's luck had not been good. He was "snake bit," as they call it. While others were hooking and landing 100- to 200-pound tuna, Itano was hooking sharks, snapping his lines and unbuttoning tuna.

It was late, and most of the anglers had retired for the night, but Itano kept at it. At 2 A.M. he set his hook firmly inside the lip of a large tuna. The fish raced toward the starboard bow, forcing Itano to follow along the wet and slippery walkway. As he ran along the gunwale, he slipped, banging his elbow against the railing. Before he could regain his balance, his rod was jarred loose from his grip and sailed over the side of the boat.

"I watched it splash into the water and disappear," Itano said. "Sheepishly, I explained the mishap to the skipper, Frank LoPreste, before rigging my backup outfit and returning to the stern to fish."

About 10 minutes later, Capt. LoPreste appeared at Itano's side, tapped him on the shoulder and handed him a rod with a fish hooked to the line.

"I thought he was kidding," Itano said. "I was in no mood for handouts. But when I took a closer look at the rod he was holding, I realized it was my rod— the one that had gone overboard!"

Itano took the rod and 30 minutes later reeled in a 165-pound yellowfin tuna.

He soon discovered what had happened. Another angler, George Jennings, had been fighting a fish from the bow on the opposite side of the boat when Itano's rod and reel went overboard. Itano's fish towed the trailing fishing gear under the bow and across Jennings' line. Jennings felt a sudden weight on his line, and when he reeled in he found his hook snagged to the crossbar of Itano's reel. Jennings, an ex-

Did You Know?

Tunas, like sharks, lack a swim bladder that controls buoyancy. If they stop swimming, they sink.

perienced angler, had felt nothing unusual other than the abrupt weight. Itano's reel had knocked his tuna off the hook before snagging by the crossbar. The switch had taken place instantly.

"When Capt. LoPreste first caught my attention I was annoyed," Itano said. "The last thing I wanted was charity. I was happy to land the fish, but even happier to retrieve my new tuna outfit. It was a long way to Yo's Custom Rod and Tackle Shop in Gardena, California."

Mas Itano and his wife Teri with the 165-pound yellowfin tuna that yanked Itano's rod and reel overboard and into the Pacific Ocean. Miraculously snagged deep below the surface by another angler's hook, the rod and reel were soon returned and the fish caught.

ACCIDENTAL CATCH

apt. George Gordon was operating his charter boat along the warm currents that surround the lush coastline of Maui, Hawaii. His clients were French tourists who spoke little English.

"The trip started off with a few of their favorite French songs," Gordon said, "and a bottle of red wine. The fishing was bad, and after two hours of no strikes, I decided to turn around and head back to the docks at Lahaina."

On the return trip, Gordon sighted a school of dolphins frolicking in the distance. He turned the boat and sped toward the school.

"As a boat captain, I see dolphins almost every day," Gordon said, "but it's always fascinating for a tourist to see them leap from the water or race against our bow. Dolphins are known to swim with schools of tuna, but I've never caught a tuna anywhere near them. In fact, I tend to stay away from dolphin schools unless the fishing is so bad that I feel a need to give my passengers a last-minute thrill before heading home with an empty fish box."

As they neared the school of dolphins, an outrigger rubber band snapped free and fishing line fell from a spinning reel. The fishing rod leaned low and the line descended into the water at a scorching pace. Gordon thrust the engine throttles into reverse and backed the boat toward the fish as fast as it would go. Water splashed over the transom for 10 minutes before the fish slowed and the angler began to gain line.

"We were gaining on the fish," Gordon said, "when off in the distance we saw a dorsal fin break the water. It sliced the surface and disappeared. Then we saw the splash of a large fish. As I got the gaff and gloves prepared for our mystery fish, we saw a dolphin jump near our line. I silently cursed, hoping the dolphin wouldn't interfere by tangling our line or frightening the fish. Our fish came nearer and nearer when the group of Frenchmen yelled that we had hooked a marlin."

Gordon explained to the Frenchmen that the fish was probably a tuna. He told them that marlin usually jump and because of all the dolphins, a school of tuna was more likely. But the Frenchmen were adamant and insisted that the fish was a marlin.

"The dolphin that had leaped earlier," Gordon said, "had long since disappeared and had not interfered with our line. Then, suddenly, there was another splash and another dolphin. This one was closer to the boat and did not swim away. As the angler cranked the reel the dolphin came closer to the boat."

The French angler reeled and minutes later an exhausted dolphin lay calmly at the stern, hooked firmly in the mouth by Gordon's fishing lure.

"I decided not to cut the line," Gordon said, "and instead wanted to try and remove the lure. I radioed to several nearby fishing boats for advice on how to remove the hook from the dolphin's mouth without hurting either one of us. No one knew what to do."

Gordon's boss was listening from shore on a CB radio, and radioed back with an idea. He told Gordon to kneel on the swim step and talk gently to the dolphin, meanwhile stroking the animal to assure it that everything would be all right. Once the dolphin was calm, Gordon could carefully cut the hook off at the barb and release the animal unharmed.

"I thought he was joking," Gordon said, "but he was serious. Slowly, and with great anxiety, I climbed down from the flybridge and into the cockpit. I stepped over the side of the transom and braced myself on the swim step. Not more than two feet away was a heavily breathing, frightened dolphin with a hook lodged into the right side of her mouth."

Gordon spoke softly and petted the dolphin as if it were his Irish Setter. The dolphin relaxed, and Gordon slowly reached inside its mouth and began to cut the barb from the hook. The large row of flat teeth ominously surrounded his bare hand.

"The clippers were dull," Gordon said, "and the barb was made from stainless steel. I thought the dolphin would get impatient with my hand in her mouth. I knew the wound was painful, but she was trusting and just lay there patiently until I was through cutting. After I cut the barb from the hook, I continued to stroke her back and talk to her. Then I gently eased out the hook. She hesitated for a moment, and quickly swam away."

Gordon deeply inhaled the salty air as the Frenchmen celebrated the successful release.

"I've never heard of a dolphin getting hooked," Gordon said. "They're usually too smart for that. This one just made a mistake. Maybe she was sick or injured, or even starving. Whatever the reasons, I was just happy I was able to free her."

DID YOU KNOW?

The most poisonous fish in the world is the death puffer. A delicacy in Japan, the death puffer inhabits the Red Sea and the Indo-Pacific waters. The poison of the death puffer is 200,000 times stronger than curare, the deadly plant poison placed on arrow tips by natives of South America. Fatalities from eating an improperly filleted death puffer occur within two hours of ingestion.

HEAD OVER HEELS

It seems that fishermen really will do anything to catch a fish. Especially if it means getting offshore to do it—rubber dinghies, motorized surfboards and now the sailboard.

Windfishing is easy if you know how to windsurf, have impeccable balance and don't mind the chance of being thrown from your board at the strike.

"It's a perfect alternative to sitting on the beach waiting for the wind to pick up," explained Tom Peach, one of Hawaii's premier windfishermen. "Windfishing allows you to work the reefs and surf

Tom Peach wind-
fishing near
the island of Oahu,
Hawaii.

Courtesy Hawaii Fishing News

lines where *papio* and *ulua* love to feed. You can get into areas that boats can't reach. There's never any engine noise to scare the fish away, and under those conditions anything can happen."

Peach was windfishing one day on the famed North Shore of the island of Oahu. A six-foot shore break made sailing out difficult, but after several attempts Peach broke through the large waves and onto a calm, flat sea. Rigging his line with a teaser bird and a "Rebel Windcheater" lure, he began trolling the reefs outside the surf line.

> **66I knew it was a big ulua, and they're known to dive into holes or under ledges to cut lines. My only chance was to stop the fish before he disappeared down into the coral.99**

An hour had passed without a strike when Peach's board came to a sudden stop. Like a cyclist who mistakenly pulls his front brake, Peach was flung forward over the board.

"I couldn't believe a fish had stopped my board!" Peach said. "The drag on my 9/0 reel was set fairly strong, but I'd never expected a hit like that."

Peach splashed back to his windsurfer, straddled the board and gripped the arching rod. With the line still spinning from the reel, he heaved back, hoping to stop the fish's descent.

"I knew it was a big *ulua*," Peach said, "and they're known to dive into holes or under ledges to cut lines. My only chance was to stop the fish before he disappeared down into the coral. I guess it was my lucky day."

The fish slowed, then stopped just short of the reef. Peach pulled firmly on the rod and for the next 45 minutes battled the stubborn fish. Three times it came to leader, and all three times it sped back down toward the safety of the coral.

"That third run was his last," Peach said. "When I brought him on board, I couldn't believe I had really landed him. He was a monster *ulua*. He'd hit my lure so hard, and it was so deep in his throat, that I couldn't retrieve it until I filleted him."

The *ulua* weighed 35 pounds. It was the largest fish Peach had ever caught while windfishing—and possibly the largest ever caught that way.

Peach has caught a lot of fish since then, and windfishing has continued to increase in popularity. There are a growing number of sailpower fishing tournaments each year in Hawaii, and more worldwide.

And as the sport continues to grow, so too should the opportunities for bigger fish. Gear and techniques will adapt to the challenges of boardfishing. Windfishermen will venture farther from shore in search of greater game and of greater challenge.

And then, one day, it will happen. A billfish will strike, and if a 35-pound *ulua* can knock an angler from a board, imagine what the billfish might do.

"I don't know," Peach said, "but in the future I might tie myself to the mast post—just in case."

GRUELING BATTLES

37 HOURS ON ROD AND REEL

It was just after noon on July 12, 1989. Bob Ploeger, his wife Darlean and fishing guide Dan Bishop sat in the drift boat floating down Alaska's Kenai River. They were enjoying their first trip to Alaska and their first time salmon fishing. Half a day of fishing was all they had planned. Two days later, exhausted and bewildered, they would wonder what had happened.

"We'd fished all morning," Ploeger explained, "and I hadn't had a strike. Darlean had hooked a couple of small fish, but that was all. At about noon, Dan Bishop rowed us out into the center of the river and anchored the boat so that he could eat lunch.

"Darlean and I kept fishing, and about the time Dan finished his sandwich I had a hit. It was the hardest hit I'd ever felt. I pulled back hard and set the hook, and for the next two hours I fought the

fish from the anchored boat. Then the fish took off out of its hole and went downstream as fast as he could go. Dan pulled up the anchor, lifted the paddles and began rowing in pursuit."

It was a frantic run for the three anglers. The salmon was swimming downcurrent faster than Bishop could paddle. Line kept spinning from the reel. The fish wasn't tiring, and Ploeger watched helplessly as the thin metal spool began to show beneath the 30-pound monofilament. Desperate to stop the fish, he pressed his thumb down over the line. The fish slowed, turned, and swam back upstream.

"We were relieved to have turned the fish," Ploeger said, "until we saw the island in the middle of the river. The fish was going up the opposite side of it and against the current. Bishop tried to follow, but the current was too strong. I was sure we'd lose the fish."

Suddenly the line stopped flowing from the reel. Once around the island, the salmon had paused to rest in some rapids. Relieved, Bishop paddled to the island and flagged down a motorized skiff. He and Ploeger quickly switched boats and drove upriver to the rapids. After a few tugs on the line, the salmon darted away from the rapids, turning back the way it had come. Darlean remained on the island with the owners of the motorized skiff and later returned to camp.

Four hours into the fight, Ploeger's fish had moved more than a mile downriver and was across from the docks where the day of fishing had begun. It was there, after sulking in the mud for 30 minutes, that the salmon first jumped. It was a giant fish, the largest salmon any of them had ever seen.

The next 30 hours were torment. The salmon was strong and stubborn, staying on the bottom and downcurrent through most of the fight. Ploeger kept pressure on the line and remained patient.

During the first night Ploeger and Bishop switched to a third boat with greater fuel capacity. A crowd had gathered along the shore of the Kenai, and many of the local charter captains were congregating on the river offering their assistance.

Also during the night media began to arrive with camera equipment and more boats. Reporters and photographers were allowed on board to interview Ploeger and record his battle with the mammoth salmon. At 10:30 P.M. the fish surfaced once more, then settled back in the mud. The night dragged on. The guides slept in rotation while Ploeger waited for daybreak.

By dawn, nothing had changed. Ploeger pulled, but the fish would not move. The river was only seven to eight feet deep so Bishop, frustrated and without any options, raised an oar into the air, leaned over the water and stabbed down at the shallow riverbed. He banged the muddy floor, attempting to scare the fish. Ploeger yanked and Bishop pounded, but the salmon hardly moved.

Between 5 o'clock that morning and 8:00 that

DID YOU KNOW?

A 3½-foot shark was found whole inside the belly of a 12-foot swordfish. More surprising still are the frequent findings in swordfish stomachs of up to 7½-foot ribbonfishes, those odd-looking, eel-like dwellers of the abyssal sea.

night, they had moved the fish only 100 yards.

By this time local radio stations had arrived and set up remote broadcasting from the shoreline. Many more spectators had also arrived, swelling the banks of the Kenai to capacity. At 8:30 P.M. a radio station announced over loudspeakers that Ploeger had broken the Guinness world record for the longest fight on rod and reel—32 hours and 5 minutes. The onlookers cheered their approval.

Five more hours passed before the fish made its final run. It darted toward shore, and the camera crew, still aboard, shone their lights into the water. The fish was exhausted. Hovering a few feet beneath the water, it approached the river's edge.

The banks of the Kenai are steep and the water only a few feet deep. The salmon hit the steep edge and stopped. Bishop yelled for Ploeger to yank back to try to raise the fish, but the salmon didn't move.

Bishop made a difficult decision. It would be risky to try to scoop the fish from the bottom, but an even greater risk to miss the opportunity to capture the cornered fish. Ploeger had been fighting for more than 37 hours and was near exhaustion. The reel's gear was wearing, and the hook could work free any moment.

Bishop and another guide each handled a net—one three feet in diameter, the other four. They corralled the fish, boxing it in, sensing victory. The water swirled along the shore when one of the nets brushed Ploeger's leader. The line broke, the rod snapped back and the plug fell from the salmon's mouth.

Both guides fought desperately to scoop the salmon into the nets. But the river bottom was covered with rocks, and each time they pushed, the nets snagged and the boat slid farther away. Suddenly, the current caught the fish and swept it around the nets and into the murky water.

Ploeger stood in the boat, staring helplessly into the river. The fish he had worked so hard for was free. The guides threw their nets down in disgust, and the camera crew shut off the lights. The battle was over. The salmon had won.

> **Ploeger had broken the Guinness world record for the longest fight on rod and reel—32 hours and 5 minutes.**

ANGLER AND SKIPPER FOR 17½ HOURS

"Swordfish!" David Denholm shouted, dashing to the bait tank. His wife Nicole reeled in the lures as Scott, their deckhand, turned the boat toward the fish. It was a Friday, midday, and they were aboard their 44-foot sportfisher *Espadon*, four hours from the coast of southern California.

Denholm rigged a large mackerel and flung it over the side. It was a perfect cast. He handed the rod to Nicole, who anxiously awaited her first swordfish strike.

"The fish hit the bait twice with his bill," Denholm said, "and cherry-picked it off the hook. We put out another bait, and he cherry-picked it again."

Denholm tossed out a third bait, but the swordfish was suddenly uninterested. He retrieved the bait and tried again, six or seven times, but the fish wouldn't strike.

"We didn't have many choices and couldn't just leave him," Denholm said, "so I decided to try a lighter outfit. The water that day was clear, and we could see the fish. He had to weigh a good 250 pounds. I knew the consequences of using lighter gear, especially with a swordfish, but I put away the 80-pound stuff and grabbed a 30."

Nicole was hesitant about battling a swordfish on such light tackle, so David took the rod. On the second cast, the swordfish swallowed the bait.

"I hit him hard," Denholm said, "with a half-dozen full backward swings. He didn't particularly respond, but I knew we were hooked. I could feel the tension."

Scott, who had never captained the *Espadon* before, knew this was no time to learn. A second set of boat controls was located on the starboard deck, allowing Denholm, who was holding the rod in one hand and the throttle in the other, to work the boat and the fish together.

"It was challenging," Denholm said, "but it was also an advantage. As the angler, I knew where the fish was and what he was doing. As the captain, I didn't worry about errors in communication. It wasn't easy, though, and it got tougher as the fight went on."

An hour passed before the swordfish surfaced. Denholm increased the drag and reversed the boat. The fish was soon within gaffing range, but as Scott stepped onto the swim step and reached out with the gaff, a ripple of water from the transom momentarily blurred his vision. He lunged down and scooped up with the gaff, catching the fish in the tail.

"The swordfish took off like a rocket," Denholm

David Denholm, shown here after another grueling battle, this time with a record yellowfin tuna. Caught on 20-pound line, the tuna took 18½ hours to land and is the largest ever landed at that line class in California waters.

Courtesy David Denholm

CHANNEL ISLANDS
INVITATIONAL
BROADBILL TOURNAMENT

ALLISON
FISH   DATE
Y.F. TUNA   10-21-83

OFFICIAL WEIGHING STATION

ANGLER DAVID DENHOLM
WEIGHT 183½ TIME 18 hrs 23 min
TACKLE 20# DACRON

said. "Scott tried to hold him, but the gaff wasn't solid and ripped free. I could see chunks of the fish floating 10 or 15 feet below the surface."

Wounded and boat-shy, the swordfish remained deep. Denholm stood with his back to the controls, watching the line angle over the stern. With his left hand he held the rod firm against his gut. With his right, he alternated reeling and steering. He fought patiently, determined to beat one of the most relentless fighters in the sea.

> **66Denholm fought patiently, determined to beat one of the most relentless fighters in the sea.99**

Six hours later, near sunset, the swordfish finally rose into the prop wash. Its color had turned to brown, and Denholm could see the large gaff hole in its side. Scott waited for the leader. Nicole hovered with the video camera. But the fish came no closer. The sun set and darkness fell.

"As the night progressed," Denholm said, "the temperature dropped. I was soaking wet from backing down across the evening chop and could not generate a scenario in my mind as to just how this fight was going to end. I don't remember the minutes passing—just the hours. I don't recall going past midnight into Saturday morning, and even though I hadn't eaten for almost 24 hours, I wasn't hungry.

"I worked hard on the fish all the time. It was not a matter of hanging on. It was a matter of taking the tackle to the limit as much as possible.

It was a mental game of constantly trying to figure out his weak spots, concentrating on how to outsmart him, and being ready when and if he made a mistake."

The battle dragged. Scott remained in the cockpit, checking the radar screen, and checking and rechecking the gaffs. Nicole went below to sleep for a few hours.

Throughout the night the fish had come close. He would come as far as the quartz deck lights, but no farther. The lights were bright, creating a wall between the boat and the fish. Denholm struggled to stay alert. Any slack in the line, any wrong move with the boat, and the swordfish would escape. Daybreak, Denholm hoped, would end the standoff.

At 5:15 Nicole emerged from the salon with a change of clothes for her husband. Denholm was cold and wet, and the new clothes were a refreshing sight.

"As I contemplated the best way to change my clothes without giving up the rod," Denholm said, "the fish initiated one of his many runs. I stood pat as usual, and without warning the line came slack. I announced, 'It's over,' and reeled in the line.

"As the broken line came in, I looked toward the horizon and saw Saturday's fishing fleet on its way out. Our overhead lights were shining down on me and I felt isolated, like none of it was real. When the end of the line came through the water, I could see the leader approach without a hook. I lifted the rod and inspected the frayed, worn leader. Another broadbill had won."

Denholm plotted the course for Newport Beach, surrendered the wheel to Nicole and went below to sleep and to dream about the next swordfish.

AGAINST ALL ODDS

For 15 years actor Willie Aames had scoured the globe in search of marlin. And in 15 years he had never caught one. His luck changed in October of 1990, on the last day of the 10th Annual Bisbee's Black & Blue Marlin Jackpot Tournament in Cabo San Lucas, Mexico.

"We caught a 300-pound black marlin and a small blue the first day of the tournament," Aames said, "and a striper on the second. We were in third place and needed a big fish to put us in front."

Aames was fishing aboard the *Leigh Ann*, a 32-foot Blackfin skippered by Capt. Tony Nungaray with Eben Brown and Juan Garcia Passett serving as deckhands. By midmorning the group was trolling the Gorda Banks, searching for their winning fish.

The $200,000 black marlin and the winning team. From right to left behind slate: Juan Garcia Passett, Willie Aames (angler), Eben Brown and Capt. Tony Nungaray.

Courtesy Larry Dunmire

"At 10:15 A.M. I looked up," Aames said, "and asked the Lord for a fish. There was a feeling I had, I don't know what it was, but I just knew something was going to happen."

The minutes passed slowly. Aames held the line and watched the bait. Fifteen minutes after asking for his fish, he got one.

"I yelled for Tony to put us in neutral, free-spooled the rod and jumped into the chair," Aames said. "When I slammed the reel into gear, the rod bent to the rail and the line went smoking out. I knew the fish had to be big."

Aames was still in the chair 12 hours later. His legs had cramped and gone numb. His hands and fingers were blistered. The fish had come close, up to the double line several times, but each time Nungaray was forced to move ahead or risk chaffing the line against the swim step.

"We couldn't get the fish all the way up," Aames explained. "Each time we had her close, the line touched the swim step and Tony had to gun the boat. It happened eight or nine times, and each time it spooked the fish and she took off. We just couldn't get her to the surface."

The odds of landing the marlin worsened by the hour. One of the two gears inside the reel froze early in the fight, and sometime during the night the drag began to give, forcing Aames to jam his hands into the spool to slow the loss of line. He wore no gloves, and soon his blistered hands were bruised, cut and badly swollen. The night wore on.

The Leigh Ann was without deck lights, and Capt. Joe Mike Lopez of the Top Hatt, who earlier had brought out food and water and extra fuel, idled nearby to illuminate the scene. But the clear monofilament line was difficult to see. Passett and Brown spent the night leaning against the railing, shining flashlights at the line.

The two deckhands poured water over Aames to keep him cool and gave him aspirin to ease his pain. The tremendous strain was taking its toll. During the cold, dark hours of early morning, Aames' right hand gave out, forcing him to reach across and reel with his left. Urine and saltwater chaffed his legs.

"It was a long night," Aames said. "Everything ached. I talked to God and asked for strength. He was all that kept me going."

By morning the fish had pulled them 30 miles north. La Paz loomed on the horizon. The Leigh Ann was dangerously low on fuel, and Nungaray had no choice but to stop following the fish so the Top Hatt could give them fuel. Dead in the water and located over deep canyons, the fishermen were also vulnerable to a death-dive. If the fish sounded, it could go too deep and burst its air bladder. Bringing a dead fish up from deep water would be futile. The fish would become an anchor and the line would almost certainly break.

"That was when the last run came," Aames said. "We were in neutral, and all Tony could do was watch. I jammed my hands into the spool for the last time and pushed back as hard as I could with my legs. The fish stopped and the rod tip slowly came up."

But the battle wasn't over. For the next three hours Aames strained, gaining just inches of line with each pump of the rod. Then, 21 hours after hook-up, the double line touched the roller guides,

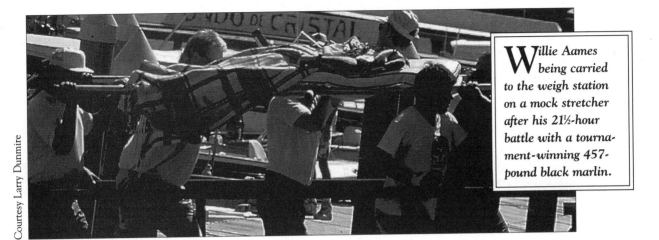

Courtesy Larry Dunmire

Willie Aames being carried to the weigh station on a mock stretcher after his 21½-hour battle with a tournament-winning 457-pound black marlin.

the swivel broke the surface for the first time, and the leader was within reach.

"I never stopped reeling," Aames said, "even when they gaffed the fish. I was too afraid to stop. I knew if I did, I wouldn't be able to start again."

Passett and Brown gaffed the fish three times before Aames moved from the fighting chair. His legs wobbled, and he fell to the deck. Passett and Brown held his arms and helped him to the railing.

"It was an emotional moment," Aames recalls. "Not sadness or tears, but a welling-up inside, a release of tension. There was also a recognition of respect that this was the fish that had taken me to the edge."

Incredibly, the fish was no longer hooked. The line had wrapped around its body and around the dorsal fin, with the hook half-hitched under the line. A hole in the fish's mouth marked the original hook-up, but sometime during the early stages of the fight the hook had pulled free.

"That explained a lot of things," Aames said.

"Why she never jumped, why we couldn't turn her, and why I felt her feeding throughout the night."

Passett and Brown tied the fish to the stern, and Nungaray turned and headed for port. Hundreds of people had gathered at the docks to see the fish. The tournament's award presentations, the richest in the world, had been postponed, and the leading teams awaited the results.

"Pulling into the harbor was something I'll never forget," Aames said. "Boats were blowing their horns and coming out to meet us. There were people crowded along the docks and lining the balconies of the hotel. Everyone was cheering and waving."

The fish, a black marlin, was hoisted up the scale. It weighed 457 pounds, enough to put Aames' team into first place. It had taken 21½ hours to land and paid more than $200,000 in prize money.

"The odds were a million to one against us," Aames said. "The reel going out . . . the fuel . . . the way the fish was hooked. It's the team that deserves the credit."

THE OLD MAN AND THE SEA—RELIVED

In the late 1950s members of Warner Brothers Studios arrived in Kailua-Kona to complete the filming of Hemingway's novelette *The Old Man and the Sea*. The small fishing village, unaccustomed to such attention, flitted with excitement. Spencer Tracy was there to play the role of the old man, Santiago. And there were cameramen, wardrobe people, scriptwriters, riggers, gaffers, and an army of maintenance men and drivers.

"They came to Kailua-Kona to finish the film," said Phil Parker, one of Hawaii's most respected big-game captains. "They had started out in the Galápagos Islands, but couldn't find a marlin big enough to film the final scenes."

To many of the townspeople, the most impressive sight—aside from Spencer Tracy—were the marlin mock-ups. Made from foam and painted to resemble the different stages of Santiago's battle, the dummy fish were indistinguishable from the real thing.

"There were three separate fish," Parker said, "each depicting a different stage of the old man's struggle with the ravaging sharks. The last fish, of course, was nothing but a head and a tail at the end of a huge skeleton. When the fake fish were placed in the water, they looked for all the world like the real thing."

During a frenzied morning of filming at the pier, a small, one-lunger-powered commercial sampan fishing boat chugged into the bay. The slow-moving boat was manned by a lone fisherman named Charley Spinney.

"Charley was an old-style, hard-working fisherman," Parker said, "who went about his business without much fanfare. Hardly anyone noticed when he stopped alongside the pier. He tied up his boat, fastened his catch to the end of a rope and hooked the rope to the chain hoist. Then he took the chain and began hoisting the fish by hand. The first thing that emerged was a huge tail that must have measured four or five feet from tip to tip. Following the tail came a huge body. Suddenly all eyes on the pier had turned and were focusing on the hoist and the fisherman. Charley kept pulling and pulling, and the fish kept coming and coming. By the time Charley got it high enough to swing onto the pier, the fish had used the entire length of the hoist."

No fish that big had ever been brought to Kailua-Kona. There was no scale large enough at the pier to weigh it, and even Charley was uncertain about what to do.

"Eventually, after a lot of tugging, pushing, and huffing and puffing," Parker said, "the huge fish was set in the bed of a pickup truck to be hauled to the platform scale at the airport. Of course, Charley had plenty of help, since by now all the Hollywood people had forgotten about their film. All their attention was focused on finding out just how much this monster weighed."

A mass of people followed Charley and his marlin to the airport, where the fish was transferred to the scale. It weighed 1,102 pounds.

"The crowd let out a roar of approval," Parker said, "and suddenly Charley was transformed from the average commercial fisherman to a fishing superstar. The mob that escorted Charley and

his fish back to the pier was just short of a ticker-tape parade."

Word of Charley's spectacular catch spread quickly, and soon all the townfolk had heard the news. The Kailua pier became a place of celebration as hundreds of local residents arrived to witness the historic catch. The fish was hoisted back up the chain for a flurry of flashing cameras.

"Charley withstood all the attention," Parker said, "and finally, after much persuasion, he began to tell his story. He had been fishing all night, alone and without success, patiently holding the handline

hoping for a strike. Then, just at dawn, a fish ate Charley's live bait and took off like an express train. Charley said he hung on for dear life.

"He said his immediate fear, since he hadn't yet seen the fish, was losing all the line. The fish was too strong for him to hold barehanded, so the first chance he got, he wrapped a turn of line around the stern post. To his amazement, he felt the stern of the boat slowly move in the direction of the fish.

"Charley explained how he suddenly had reason for concern. Not only was the fish large and powerful, and towing the boat, but it was also beginning to circle, forcing him to race around the deck changing post positions. He pulled with all his strength, and the progress was slow but steady.

"He said the fish circled the boat at least five times, and each time the circles became smaller and the angle of the line rose higher. Charley was retrieving line, but he was far from winning the battle. He had to fight through the fear of boating such a large fish alone and so far from shore. His muscles ached, and his mind became weary.

"Then a huge marlin, exhausted and turned on her side, began to emerge from the depths. Charley said his hopes soared as he pulled it closer. The giant fish, having spent herself during the hour-long struggle, was now just beyond the stern. Charley worked quickly. He held the line tightly around the post and reached for the gaff. He paused for an instant, raised the gaff into position and buried it just behind the gill plate. He said he felt his stomach turn over as he watched his huge opponent thrash and jump in a last attempt to break free of his grasp. But the rope held, and Charley quickly secured the beast with another gaff to the body.

"He grabbed another rope and tied a half hitch around the marlin's thick sword, then dropped the fish back from the boat and tied her off the stern. He slumped down onto the deck in relief and disbelief at what he had just accomplished."

As Charley told his story, a sandy-haired man appeared in the crowd. He was short and stocky, with a full beard and a sunburned face, and as he made his way through the crowd toward Charley, he smiled in admiration.

The man was Spencer Tracy. He stepped up to Charley and shook his hand firmly. Then he threw his arms around the fisherman, hugged him and said in a commanding voice, "Hell, I'm not the old man of the sea. Here's the old man of the sea!"

"Charley had a great deal of respect for Spencer Tracy," Parker said, "and to this day I'm sure he can still hear those words."

26 HOURS ON THE STICK

Ron LeGrand and his wife Jeanne woke before dark, excited about the day of fishing ahead. They left the docks at Huntington Harbor, California, and by daybreak had reached Catalina Island, 15 miles from the coast.

They spent the day trolling lures and by mid-afternoon were 20 miles northwest of Catalina, near the east end of Santa Barbara Island.

"We had a few strikes," LeGrand said, "but nothing stayed on. I don't know why, but I decided to put out a great big orange jig on the center line,

as a teaser more than anything. A short time later, we hooked a marlin on that lure."

LeGrand cleared the remaining lines and prepared for the struggle. Jeanne remained at the controls and drove the boat.

"It was a strange fight," LeGrand said. "I got the fish within 40 yards of the boat many times, and then he would stop as if he'd hit a brick wall. He would start out again, not fast, just slowly chugging off the line. The frustrating part was that I was using 50-pound line and couldn't stop him."

A successful ending this time as Ron LeGrand congratulates his son Alex on a job well done (note the striped marlin lying across the transom).

Courtesy Ron LeGrand

The marlin made repeated runs, stripping almost all 350 yards of line from the spool. Again and again Jeanne reversed the boat toward the fish, but by nightfall nothing had changed.

"We had plans to go to Avalon that night," LeGrand said, "and as dusk fell I knew Jeanne was disappointed. I was, too. We'd caught plenty of marlin before, but none had fought like this."

One explanation for the prolonged battle was a foul hook-up. The water that day was uncommonly clear, and more than once the marlin had been in sight. The LeGrands could see the lure dangling from the side of the fish's forehead.

As the battle continued, friends called with suggestions and support. The LeGrands tried everything, even slacking the line to confuse the fish. Nothing worked.

"Nighttime was difficult," LeGrand said. "This was our first boat, and it wasn't fully equipped. There were no deck lights and no fighting chair. The cabin light was all we had, and it wasn't much help."

As the night progressed, lights appeared and disappeared on the horizon, some closer than others. During one period, a commercial freighter festooned in running lights seemed destined to end the battle by ramming the small boat, but veered to the outside in time to avoid disaster.

At daybreak, after 15 hours without food or rest, a call came over the radio. One of their close friends, Dr. Gordy Bateman, offered to bring out his son Jim as a deckhand.

"We were happy to have another body aboard," LeGrand said, "to help when it came time to gaff the fish. We were both pretty tired by then. Jim also brought some much-needed food. It was difficult to eat standing up and holding the rod, but I managed to get some down and it helped."

By late afternoon, the strain on LeGrand was obvious. His sense of direction languished. Depth perception became hazy at best. Dizzy spells turned to hallucinations.

"It was about 6 o'clock and the sun was still shining when the fish made his final move," LeGrand said. "As usual, he was below the boat, but this time I was too tired to do anything about it. There was maybe 100 feet of line out when he moved across our transom. The line nicked the propellers and it was all over. I wound up the limp line and laid down the rod. Twenty-six-plus hours for a fish, and then it was over just like that."

The battle's effect on LeGrand lingered. Twenty-six hours of exertion and lack of sleep had thrust him deep into delirium, and during the three-hour trip back to harbor his hallucinations intensified.

"It was a long ride home, and one very vivid memory I have is seeing a crew of university guys rowing across the water. This was 9 o'clock at night in the open ocean, and I was sure they were there. But it was all in my imagination. I don't know how, but later, through the blur, I managed to get the boat on the trailer.

"The next morning I awoke on the couch, where I had passed out. I ached everywhere, and my hands were blistered. I felt terrible and never wanted to fish again."

Two days after the ordeal, LeGrand's desire to fish returned. He began cleaning the boat and discovered the engines had never been shut off. They idled on the trailer until the fuel tanks emptied. It was a final reminder of the fight that would not end.

REVENGE OF THE FISH

THUMBING FOR TROUT

Robert Lindsey sat at the bow of the ski boat, watching his daughter busily playing at the stern. It was an ideal summer day, and Lindsey and a group of friends were boating on the Flaming Gorge Reservoir, a world-class trout destination that meanders along the Wyoming/Utah state line.

The midday boat ride had been pleasant and uneventful. Suddenly, the slow wake of a distant houseboat welled up and crashed over the ski boat's bow. The wall of water careened into Lindsey, knocking him off balance.

"All I remember is the wave coming over the boat," Lindsey said. "It went right over my back and filled the boat with water. One of my friends' daughters was sitting up front with me, and she was covered with water. Her mother was screaming, and as I regained my balance and bent down to help the girl, another wave came over the bow and threw me over the side."

The boat traveled over Lindsey, pinning him beneath the hull. He was upside down and moving headfirst toward the spinning propeller. His eyes were open, and he saw the bottom of the boat passing overhead.

"I knew I had to get out of there," Lindsey said. "I was trying to swim out from under the boat when I felt my hand go through the propeller. It's hard to explain the feeling. I didn't feel any pain, but I knew immediately that my hand was in bad shape."

Lindsey kicked hard to distance himself from the boat, but the twirling propeller caught his right leg and tore a deep gash from his knee to his foot. Moments later, dazed and bloodied, he surfaced.

"The first thing I saw was my index finger and my middle finger lying alongside my wrist," Lindsey said. "The only thing holding them on was a little piece of skin. Blood was squirting everywhere, and I couldn't see my thumb."

The boat had partially sunk and all the pas-

Courtesy Blake Robinson

The gutted mackinaw trout and Robert Lindsey's severed thumb, found inside the fish's belly.

sengers were in the water. The children were ac-
counted for while Lindsey treaded water nearby.
He was without a life jacket and in shock.

"I was losing a lot of blood," Lindsey said, "and
I was beginning to feel pretty weak. Finally, one of
the guys swam over to help me. I latched onto his
life jacket with my good hand and held on.

"There was a boat off in the distance, and we
started yelling and hollering as loud as we could. I
wanted out of the water real bad, and when the boat
pulled up next to us I yanked myself out of the water
with my one good hand."

Lindsey spent 17 days in the hospital and underwent reconstructive surgery to attach his two severed fingers. His thumb was gone, and his leg
required numerous staples and stitches to repair the
jagged wound.

Seven months after the accident, Lindsey's wife
was told of a local newspaper article recounting a
story about an angler who had discovered a human
thumb in the belly of a trout. Blake Robinson had
been ice fishing on the Flaming Gorge Reservoir
when, late in the afternoon, he landed a six-pound
mackinaw trout. The fish was a keeper, measuring
just under the 26-to-36-inch slot limit set by the
state to protect the lake's trout population. Robinson stopped fishing and immediately filleted the
trout on the frozen lake.

"When I cleaned the fish," he said, "I noticed
that the belly looked like it had something in it.
We'd been fishing with bullheads all day, and
we wanted to see what else the fish had been eating. I cut open the trout's belly and out fell
the thumb. At first it didn't register that it was a
human thumb."

The thumb was well preserved, and after recovering from the initial shock Robinson wrapped it in
a piece of cellophane. He marked the location on
the ice with a red flag and took the thumb to the
local sheriff's office. The sheriff filed a report and
delivered the thumb to the local coroner, who
placed it in a cooler.

"After reading the newspaper article," Lindsey
said, "I called the coroner and told him I thought
the thumb might be mine. He thought I was some
kind of practical joker and wanted to know if I'd
filed a report about it. I told him I had—but only
on the Utah side of the lake, where the accident
had occurred. The report was never sent to the
Wyoming side, so nobody knew about it over there.
The coroner checked everything out and called me
back about two weeks later. He asked if I could come
identify the thumb."

Lindsey obtained the x-rays from his hand surgery and went to the morgue to meet the coroner.
The thumb was removed from the cooler, and it
perfectly matched Lindsey's hand and the x-rays of
his wound.

"The x-rays were important," Lindsey said,
"because I had never been fingerprinted. Everything fit perfectly. Even the cuts from the propeller matched."

The coroner was satisfied and released the
thumb to Lindsey, who keeps it in a jar of formalde-
hyde on a shelf in his closet.

"I was shocked when I heard about an angler
finding a human thumb in a fish," Lindsey said.
"The acid in a fish's stomach can dissolve a fishhook
in a few days, so the angler must have hooked the
trout within a few hours after it ate my thumb."

SPEARED

Bob Fitzgerald didn't realize how lucky he was. The white marlin that speared his thigh had somehow missed the femoral artery.

"My wife and I were fishing off Andros Island in the Bahamas," Fitzgerald explained, "with Mike and Sunny Wirtz, owners of the 91-foot yacht *Black-hawk*, and our friends Bob and Barbara Carlson. It was 11 o'clock in the morning, and I had just caught our first marlin of the trip. I stayed in the fighting chair and waited for one of the crew members to gaff the fish and bring him aboard."

It was a small white marlin, exhausted by the fight. But as it cleared the stern the weary fish unex-

pectedly came to life. "I remember seeing the fish come over the transom and flip into the air. One minute he was calm, and the next minute he was a wild animal heading straight for me. It happened so fast, I couldn't get out of the chair. I just jerked to the side as far as I could and covered my face with my arms."

The marlin crashed into the boat, driving its bill through Fitzgerald's thigh. Everyone on board watched in horror as the fish ripped its bill from his leg and flopped wildly about the deck.

"As the bill came out," Fitzgerald said, "the barbs pulled muscle out through the hole. It was terrible to look at, but it plugged the wound and stopped the bleeding."

Those in the cockpit scrambled for cover while the captain radioed for help.

"There were some doctors around," Capt. Hillard Hardy recalled, "but they were out fishing and wouldn't be back at the dock until late that afternoon. We cleaned the wound and turned toward shore, but Bob insisted we stay out so the rest of the gang could fish. I didn't like it, but he was adamant. The leg seemed okay, so we moved him to the upper deck and kept close watch over him in case the wound got any worse. Bob was a good patient. All he wanted was a fresh martini and some more fishing."

The decision turned out to be a good one. Sunny and Jane hooked into a double strike, and Mike landed a large blue marlin. Fitzgerald, his leg numb and swollen, watched from above, nursing martinis and cheering his friends' good fortune.

But by the time they arrived at the docks, Fitzgerald's leg was too stiff to move. Dr. Gordon Hill, an orthopedic surgeon from Miami, had been informed of the injury and was waiting at the dock.

"The leg was badly bruised and was bleeding internally," Hill said, "but the major arteries and the bone were not damaged. He was very fortunate."

Hill cleaned the wound, administered antibiotics and painkillers, and suggested that Fitzgerald get medical attention in the United States. After a day at sea and a long flight from the Bahamas to Illinois, Fitzgerald arrived in Chicago and went immediately to his own physician, Dr. Blazek. By now the leg had turned dark purple.

"Had the marlin hit his femoral artery," Blazek said, "Bob could have lost his leg and possibly his life. There would have been no way to stop the massive bleeding that would have ensued. A tourniquet would have been his only chance."

After weeks of therapy, Fitzgerald's leg healed. Full use of the muscles returned, and 15 years later all that remains is a small scar.

DID YOU KNOW?

The heaviest lobster ever captured weighed 44 pounds, 6 ounces. The lobster was caught near Nova Scotia, Canada, in 1977.

RATTLESNAKE ON BOARD

Kevin Jones and his fishing partner, Paul Shepherd, were anxious to catch their second bass of the day. It was early morning, and the two anglers were contestants in the 1992 American Bass Association's Team tournament held at Lake Castaic in southern California. Shepherd had caught their first bass, a qualifying 3½-pound largemouth that was promptly placed in the boat's live well.

"We were feeling pretty good," Jones said. "It was still early in the morning, and we had a good fish in the live well. We needed five more to make the limit, so we headed into a nearby cove to see what we could find."

Shepherd stood at the bow, controlling the boat with the foot pedal and fishing a spinner bait. Jones was at the stern, working a crank-bait deep. Slowly they fished the water and moved deeper and deeper into the cove.

"I caught a dink," Jones said, "probably no more than 10 inches long, and as I released it I heard a splash near the shore. I thought maybe Paul had hooked a fish. When I looked up toward the bank, which was about 50 feet away, I saw something in the water. It was moving and coming our way."

Jones made another cast, and Shepherd hollered, "Snake!" Expecting Shepherd to move the boat elsewhere, Jones quickly reeled in his lure. Instead, Shepherd calmly resumed fishing.

"Paul is from Oregon," Jones said, "and he had dealt with snakes before, so I figured he knew what he was doing. I decided not to worry about it. I made another cast, and suddenly Paul said in a tense voice, 'Kevin, that's a rattlesnake!'"

Shepherd quickly reeled in his fishing line and changed the course of the boat away from the snake. Jones also retrieved his line and remained at the stern, nervously watching the rattlesnake.

"He was about 25 feet from us when we changed course," Jones said, "and he changed course right with us. Paul got a little nervous and hit the trolling motor to full speed. I thought that would do it, but within seconds the snake was right next to the boat."

Jones raised his expensive bass rod and thrashed at the water between the rattlesnake and the boat. But the snake was not deterred. "He wrapped him-

> **❝It was like a nightmare. The rattlesnake had come back to life, and I knew then that he was after us.❞**

self around our big engine, and I was sure he wanted inside the boat. Paul was worried, too. He kept yelling, 'Don't let that snake on this boat!' "

Jones tossed his pole aside and grabbed the fishnet. He swung the net like a baseball bat but couldn't hit the snake.

"He was curled down in a little crevice," Jones said, "and I couldn't quite get at him. Finally I got brave and moved in close. I stood on the step near the back of the boat and poked the handle of the net into his body, and each time he would strike out and try to bite it."

Panicked and frustrated, Jones reared back and jabbed down hard at the snake. As the net came down, his foot slipped and he fell to the floor of the boat less than a foot from the snake's head. He was down for only a second, but he could see the snake looking right at him.

"He struck out at my face," Jones said, "but he was coiled so tightly around the engine cables that he couldn't get any distance on his strikes."

Jones sprang from the floor and snatched the net. He aimed carefully and struck the snake square in the midsection. For the first time, the snake flinched. "The spot where I hit him was as big around as my calf. He started to uncoil, and at first I couldn't tell if he was coming in or going out. Luckily he went out."

The snake dropped into the water, and for the first time Jones had a clear view of his body. He swung hard and fast with the net and struck the snake across the head. The snake went limp and sank beneath the surface.

"When he went limp," Jones said, "he straightened out completely, and I said to Paul, 'My God, look at the size of him!' That snake was at least six feet long, and Paul told me he counted eight or nine buttons on his tail."

After the snake disappeared, Jones turned and looked at Sheperd in disbelief. When he turned back around, the snake was coming straight at them.

"It was like a nightmare," Jones said. "The rattlesnake had come back to life, and I knew then that he was after us. He swam to the side of the boat and started coming out of the water. That's when I lost it. I grabbed the net again and started flailing with everything I had. I must have hurt him, because he turned away, swam to the opposite side of the cove and coiled up underneath a tree."

Afterward, in another part of the lake, Jones and Shepherd discussed the experience.

"We realized that all we had to do was start the big engine and drive away," Jones said. "But we were too panicked. Plus, we never imagined the snake would come after us in the first place."

Thirty minutes later the two anglers resumed fishing, and that night they were awarded the 15th-place check in the tournament.

"We really felt like we'd earned it," Jones said. "The fishing hadn't been very good, but we finished in the money. Now, whenever I'm fishing, I carry a big stick. It can get real spooky out there once you've had a rattlesnake that big chase your boat and try to come in after you."

DID YOU KNOW?

There are more than 40,000 different fishes, nearly twice the number of all other vertebrates combined.

LUCKY TO BE ALIVE

P aul Claus felt the water rushing by and knew he would soon drown. The heavy chair he was strapped to was bolted to the engine cover and both were sinking fast. And 800 pounds of blue marlin towed all of it straight down.

It was November of 1984, and Claus had hooked his first marlin. He and Glenn Van Valin, owner of the 26-foot fishing boat *Karma*, had fished together many times before. This was a day they would never forget.

"Bait had been easy to find," Claus says, "and by 6:30 in the morning we were hooked up. The fish hit immediately, even before Glenn could get the line in the outrigger. I jumped into the chair and slipped into the harness. It was loose, but I never had a chance to tighten it. There was also a seat belt to keep me snug in the chair, and when the marlin got close Glenn told me to unsnap it in case he needed my help. Unsnapping the belt and wearing a loose harness probably saved my life."

One end of a thick, ⅝″ nylon rope was tied to the base of the fighting chair, the other end to the flying gaff. The fighting chair was fastened to the engine cover, and the engine cover to the deck. Stainless steel held everything in place. As Van Valin reached over the transom, preparing to gaff the fish, neither could have expected what happened next.

"The first thing I remember is the explosion of fish and water," Claus said. "Then I felt this tremendous jerk and I was flying through the air. I remember the panic as I tried to grab things on my way out of the boat—Glenn, the railing, anything to save my life."

> **❝I thought I was going to die, and a lot of things went through my mind. Then I had this overpowering urge to fight.❞**

Claus didn't know it then, but the marlin had ripped the four-by-six-foot engine cover from its bolts, carrying it and the fighting chair overboard. "When I hit the water, I could see junk all around me. There was incredible chaos, and the pressure was enormous—not from the depth, but from the speed and the resistance of the water. It felt like a speedboat was pulling me headfirst under the water. I couldn't move.

"I thought I was going to die, and a lot of things went through my mind. Then I had this overpowering urge to fight. It was a stupid way to die, and I got mad. I started struggling to slide my arm under the harness. I remember getting it free and sticking it out. Then everything stopped. There was no more chaos, no more pressure, just silence and darkness."

Claus was near death. He could see hazy sunlight in one direction and darkness in the other. He surged toward the light. His lungs tore at his throat. His head throbbed. His vision began to narrow.

His wife Donna, who had been driving the boat, was hysterical. Van Valin, who had been struck by the chair and the engine cover, was dazed and bleeding. Both were in shock as they searched the water for signs of Claus.

"When I didn't think I could go any further," Claus said, "I looked up and saw the hull of the boat. It was a struggle to stay conscious, but somehow I made it. That first breath of air felt like a second chance at life. Glenn was all banged up, and Donna was crying. That's when I realized how lucky I'd been. They helped me up, but I couldn't stand. I found later that my inner ears were filled with water."

Van Valin had broken some ribs and needed 18 stitches to repair the wounds to his head. Claus had no visible injuries. Although the pressure of his descent had forced water through his ears, the eardrums were not damaged.

"A few days after the accident," Claus said, "I went back out with scuba gear to gauge my depth. I took my mask off underwater and looked up at the boat. I estimated my deepest point at 80 feet, 30 feet when I first saw the hull of the boat.

"Donna told me later that I had been underwater for more than a minute and a half. A few more seconds and I never would have made it."

SQUASHED BY A 150-POUND LEAPING RAY

The water off north Florida's St. Theresa beach was flat and calm. Only a slight ripple marred the surface. Rick Carroll sat near the rear of his 14-foot Evinrude, running her at full speed. His sons, Carlton and John Adam, stood at the bow, enjoying the ride. Bill Piotrowski, Carroll's close friend, sat in the center of the boat. They were in the Gulf of Mexico headed for Turkey Point Flats, a shoal two miles away. It was early morning, and they would soon be trolling for sea trout.

Courtesy Capt. Snooks Fuller

Caught in 1960 in Otehei Bay, off the north island of New Zealand, this 425-pound stingray dwarfs the existing IGFA all-tackle world record. The enormous ray, measuring 8½ feet from head to tail and 6½ feet from fin to fin, was landed by Bill Bendall (at left) while at anchor aboard Capt. Snooks Fuller's charter boat Lady Doreen. At right is Bendall's fishing mate, George Mandeno.

They were streaking across the water when the boat was suddenly jolted. Carroll, whose vision was blocked by Piotrowski, cut the engine, certain they had hit a buoy. But there was no buoy. Instead, draped across the bow was a spotted eagle ray weighing roughly 150 pounds. Carlton, who had been standing at the bow, lay pinned and bleeding beneath the ray.

"The ray had free-jumped," Carroll explained, "and came down in our boat. His huge wings were flapping over both sides of the boat. I knew Carlton was hurt, but I didn't know how bad."

Carroll rushed to the bow, grasped the ridge of bone above the ray's eyes, and pulled. Piotrowski, whose knees had been pinned beneath the ray, pushed upward. But the ray wouldn't budge. Panicked, Carroll dropped to the floor and wedged his back under the ray's belly. With a burst of adrenaline, he moved the ray's center of gravity and slid it off the boat.

Carlton was unconscious. "When I removed his life jacket," Carroll said, "his head flopped backward. His ear was full of blood, and I thought for sure his neck was broken."

While Carroll cradled his son in his arms, Piotrowski gunned the engine and raced for shore.

"The boat had water in it from the ray," Carroll said, "and we seemed to be moving at a snail's pace. Fortunately, a faster boat was nearby and we flagged it down. Three young teenage boys pulled aside, and I jumped in holding Carlton and screamed for them to head for shore. I kept praying to God for Carlton to be all right."

When they arrived at the docks, the teenagers ran for help and returned minutes later with a doctor. The doctor treated Carlton for 45 minutes until an emergency helicopter arrived from Tallahassee.

"After the chopper took Carlton to the hospital," Carroll said, "I learned that his pulse had stopped three different times. Without the doctor's help, my son would have died."

The Lifeflight Helicopter crew flew Carlton to Tallahassee Memorial Hospital, where he lay unconscious for two days. Five days later, after recovering from a major concussion, he was released.

"By having access to a helicopter and expert medical attention," Carroll said, "we still have our precious son. And best of all, he's still a fisherman."

Five-year-old Carlton Carroll and the helicopter that helped save his life after a large ray leaped into the air and crashed down on the bow of the boat where he was standing.

Courtesy Capt. Rick Carroll

NOSE FLY

Fortunately, Bill Poyneer's rainbow trout was a trophy-size fish. Otherwise, his unpleasant experience on Mexican Hay Lake would have remained just that.

The balmy summer morning was clear when Poyneer paddled his canoe to the center of the lake, one of many sprinkled across the Indian Reservations of Arizona's White Mountains. He carried a fly rod, a tackle box and a 12-gauge shotgun in his canoe. When the fishing slowed, he planned to hunt ducks.

"Mexican Hay is shallow," Poyneer said, "only about four feet deep all the way across. I was fishing the middle of the lake when I saw a water spout over on one side. It hit a boat and flipped it over. Summer was the time of year for the little whirlwinds of sand called dust devils, and when they crossed the water they created water spouts. I knew this one was traveling my way, but I thought it would miss me."

Once he saw that it was coming right at him, Poyneer paddled frantically. But the water spout was too swift. It caught Poyneer and capsized his canoe. Poyneer retrieved his gear from the lake's shallow bottom, righted his canoe and returned to shore. "That should have been a warning," he said. "But it was early in the day and I wanted to fly-fish." He dried his gun and laid his wet clothes in the sun. Changing into dry clothes, he gathered up his fly gear and returned to the lake in a float tube.

"I hooked a big trout on my 3-weight rod," Poyneer said, "and played it for about 20 minutes. It came up a few feet away from the float tube and lay on its side. I thought it was dead."

Since he had no net, Poyneer lifted the fly rod high and pulled the trout toward the float tube. The trout was heavy, and the fly rod strained against the weight. When it was just within Poyneer's reach, the fish came to life suddenly and leaped. The fly came unhooked and snapped back at Poyneer's face. The airborne fish landed inside the float tube and flopped wildly about. Blood spilled down Poyneer's face.

"It was awful," Poyneer said. "The fly went right up my nose, and it was the first time all day that I hadn't pinched down the barb on the hook. I knew I couldn't get the fly out, so I cut the line and kicked back to shore. The trout was dead in the tube and there was blood everywhere."

Poyneer drove 35 minutes to the nearest hospital, where the fly was surgically removed from his nostril.

"All the nurses and doctors came to see the fisherman with a fly up his nose," he said. "It caused a lot of interest." Two stitches later and hours after getting hooked, he returned to the lake. "I didn't get back there until late that afternoon. By then I had to pack up and head home."

The rainbow trout measured 25 inches from nose to tail and weighed 5 pounds. It is the largest and most memorable rainbow trout Poyneer has yet caught. Today, the notorious fish is displayed proudly on a wall at Tight Lines, Poyneer's fly shop in Tucson, Arizona.

NEARLY SKEWERED

It was the first day of the marlin tournament when Chuck Knox, then head coach of the Los Angeles Rams football team, landed his first billfish. He stood in the cockpit and watched the captain and crew of the Mexican charter boat tie his fish to the stern.

They were fishing off the coast of Rancho Buena Vista, a small fishing village near the tip of Baja California where Howard Ashby, one of Coach Knox's close friends, had arranged a private fishing tournament for the players and coaches of the Rams.

"I had just caught my first marlin," Knox said, "when I saw another one jump near the left side of the boat. The guys on my team were busy helping the captain with my fish, so I climbed up the ladder to the fly bridge for a better look at the free-jumping fish. I had reached the top of the ladder when the marlin suddenly shot

out of the water and came flying over the bridge right in front of me. His bill smashed through the side of the boat, tearing a piece of wood from the fly bridge. I just stood there, afraid to move."

The marlin landed in the water on the opposite side of the boat and swam away. Everyone on board rushed to the ladder and stared into the water.

"We saw the piece of wood floating in the water," the coach continued, "so we fished it out as a memento. It had a perfect hole in the middle, where the bill had gone through."

Keith Newman, who was on the boat with Knox, used the CB radio to relay the story to Howard Ashby.

"I was on another boat," Ashby said, "when I heard the call come in. They were all pretty excited, so I knew they weren't kidding around. I'd seen marlin ram boats before, but nothing like that."

Ashby kept the splintered wood and had it mounted as the "Perennial 110 Percent Trophy," to be awarded to the winners of his annual tournament.

Sixteen years later, Knox can still see the marlin as it flew by. "It was frightening as hell," he said. "I was within a foot or so of that bill and came close to being speared. Anyone sitting on that fly bridge would have been hurt."

DID YOU KNOW?

The longest recorded flight of a flying fish occurred in 1972 in Mozambique Channel off the east coast of Africa. The fish remained airborne for 90 seconds and traveled approximately 1,214 yards.

TUNA WRECK

World War II was being waged on the battlefields of Europe when Ed Cleland climbed to the bridge of his commercial fishing boat berthed in southern California. He was a Lockheed flight inspector who flew test missions over the San Fernando Valley during the week and donned his commercial skipper's cap while searching for tuna on weekends.

As usual, the albacore were plentiful near the east end of Catalina Island, and with an average daily catch of 800 pounds Cleland was eager to begin fishing.

Eight lines were trolled—three from each outrigger and two from the stern railing. The lures were made of bone and knotted to eight 250-pound leaders. Each leader was tied to a heavy rope, which was tied to a resilient shock cord to absorb the power of a striking tuna. Most of the tuna Cleland caught off Catalina weighed 30 to 40 pounds, well within the strength of his gear.

Cleland soon found the schooling tuna. He trolled through without a strike and had begun to circle when the starboard shock cord snapped with a strike. Immediately another snapped, then another. Suddenly all eight lines were hooked to a fish. The outriggers, made from eucalyptus wood, were unaccustomed to such weight and bowed sharply toward the water.

Cleland and his deckhand moved quickly to secure the lines when a loud *crackkk!* split the air, stopping them mid-stride. A bird's nest of ropes, railings and twisted lines floated in the distance. Fish, big fish, jumped among the debris.

"All our gear was stripped clean," Cleland said. "Everything, even the railings, had been torn off the boat. I'd never seen anything like it. It really scared the hell out of us."

The fish, yellowfin or bluefin tuna, were estimated to weigh more than 100 pounds each—a full day's haul caught and lost in a matter of seconds.

WAHOO ATTACK

Lou Wiczai took his position at the stern of the 92-foot charter fishing boat *Royal Star*. He was one of more than 30 anglers deep in wahoo country, 500 miles south of Cabo San Lucas, Mexico. The island of Roca Partida, the first stop of their 16-day trip, rose solemnly in the distance, marking the location of some of the best game-fishing water in the world.

Wiczai, a burly veteran and unflagging tuna fisherman, waited with three other anglers for the signal from skipper Dave Kagawa to toss out the first lures of the trip. Kagawa had divided the anglers into teams of four, each angler trolling from the stern in half-hour increments. When the signal was given, Wiczai positioned his lure beyond the wake, and his rod jerked forward with a strike. It was the first fish of the trip.

After adding another wahoo and a small tuna

> **I looked at my arm, and all I saw was blood,"** Wiczai said. "My first thought was, 'Oh God, there goes my fishing trip.'**"**

to his sack, Wiczai was back in position trolling from the stern. This time the angler at the starboard corner was first to hook up. The boat stopped and the waiting anglers rushed the bait wells, anticipating game fish below.

Wiczai wound in his lure and lifted it from the surface. As he turned his back to change fishing rods, he glimpsed a flurry of splashes off the stern and a shadow coming toward him. Instinctively, he raised his arm to cover his face.

Mouth agape, a 40-pound wahoo smashed into his forearm. The force of the blow slammed his arm against his head, shattering his glasses. The wahoo ricocheted off, splashed back into the sea and swam away.

"I looked at my arm, and all I saw was blood," Wiczai said. "My first thought was, 'Oh God, there goes my fishing trip!'"

The wahoo, which had vaulted from the sea in pursuit of an angler's lure, had ripped its teeth into the top of Wiczai's forearm. Blood gushed from the deep three-inch gash, leaving delicate arteries exposed.

The skipper and crew rushed to Wiczai's aid, cleaning and packing the wound with fresh gauze. Within minutes they were headed toward Socorro Island, the largest island in the Revillagigedo chain and site of the only medical facility within 500 miles.

The skipper radioed ahead with the emergency report: one of his anglers, a 71-year-old diabetic with high blood pressure, had been seriously injured. The control at Socorro radioed back. The doctor was fishing but would be back for their arrival. Meanwhile, Leroy Shintaku, the second skipper aboard, radioed the United States Coast Guard. The Coast Guard responded with an emergency plane en route from San Diego.

Seven hours later, his arm bandaged and held high above his head, Wiczai arrived at Socorro. The doctor repacked his arm with fresh gauze, injected him with antibiotics and recommended a trip to a major hospital.

Wiczai was taken to the island's airport—a bare strip of land and an aged macadam airstrip covered with cracks, weeds, and occasional herds of wild goats. No lights illuminated the runway, and no control tower regulated the random flights.

The Coast Guard plane arrived at dusk, and as it came to a stop the hatchway opened and two medics exited, expecting a broken-down old man. Instead they found Wiczai, a tough ex-sailor who only wanted to return to fishing.

"I'd never caused such a fuss in all my life," Wiczai said. "I knew I was injured, but I felt just fine."

After a quick checkup, the medics put him on the plane and he was flown to the San Diego Naval Hospital. Nerves in his arm were damaged, and the wound was open to infection. Surgery was required.

A naval ambulance was waiting in San Diego when Wiczai arrived. It was 10 o'clock in the evening, 15 hours since his injury.

Wiczai underwent surgery and spent five days in the hospital recovering from his injury. Although he lost partial use of his hand, his fishing was not affected.

"I owe a lot of thanks to everyone involved," Wiczai said. "Without them, I probably wouldn't be here planning my next fishing trip."

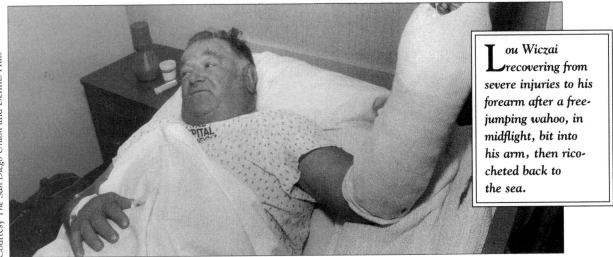

Lou Wiczai recovering from severe injuries to his forearm after a free-jumping wahoo, in midflight, bit into his arm, then ricocheted back to the sea.

FRESHWATER CROCODILES

Colin Cordingly, three-time winner of the prestigious Barramundi Classic, is one of the best-known barramundi fishermen in Australia. But with the fame comes the risk of attack by Australia's notorious freshwater crocodiles.

"If you fish barramundi," Cordingly said, "you learn to live with the crocs."

One of Cordingly's most harrowing experiences took place on the Finnis River on the west side of the Northern Territory at a water hole called Sweet's Lookout.

"It's a well-known barramundi spot," Cordingly said. "'Sweet' stands for Sweetheart, an 18-foot crocodile who used to live there. Sweetheart never attacked any anglers, but engine noises upset her."

> **Sweetheart shook the small craft in her jaws and snapped the motor in half.**

Cordingly and his friends were fishing from two 12-foot aluminum boats. As his friends rounded a bend in the river, Sweetheart emerged from the water and attacked their outboard motor. She shook the small craft in her jaws and snapped the motor in half. Then she grabbed the boat by the transom and began tearing it to pieces.

"One of my mates picked up an oar," Cordingly said, "and hit Sweetheart in the head. This made her even angrier, and she ripped the oar from his hands. My other mate was at the bow, paddling like mad to get away. As Sweetheart chewed on the oar, they came back around the bend so fast they were nearly planing the boat. Some other fishermen were close by, and they came to their rescue and towed their damaged boat to safety."

Cordingly had another frightening incident that took place years earlier during an excursion on the East Alligator River.

"The river was at about half-tide," he said, "and we were traveling at full planing speed up one of the many small creeks that flow into the outback. In this creek, the tidal water had dropped so low that its banks were about four or five feet above our heads."

Cordingly was standing at the wheel of the small outboard boat when he felt a gust of wind brush across the top of his head. He turned toward the bank and saw dirt tumbling into the creek. Then he heard a splash on the opposite side of the boat.

"The creek was only seven or eight feet wide,"

Cordingly said, "so at first I thought the falling dirt was caused by the wash from our boat. But one of my blokes was sitting in the bow facing me, and when I saw his eyes all buggered out I knew something must have happened."

Earlier that day, during high tide, an 18-foot crocodile had crawled onto the bank to sun himself and had lain there asleep until Cordingly's

engine startled him. The groggy crocodile had lunged for the safety of the water just as the boat drove by, missing Cordingly's head by inches.

"I never saw him," Cordingly said. "But if the bank of the creek had given way a little more, two tons of angry crocodile would have landed right in our boat."

POP! GOES THE DINGHY

Rob Cassady and Bill Hannah hauled the rubber dinghy down the beach to the shore of El Embarco Dorado, Mexico. They loaded their fishing gear, jumped inside and zoomed out to sea. It was October 1988, the peak of the fishing season at the East Cape.

> **When I felt the impact, I didn't know what to expect. I looked up and saw the marlin thrashing around.**

They slowed at the local wahoo grounds, a mile or so from shore, and tossed out two shiny jet-head jigs—a favorite wahoo snack. Cassady sat at the stern, holding the throttle in one hand and his fishing rod in the other. After a few passes across the grounds, a huge shadow appeared behind Cassady's jig. Seconds later the surface exploded—"Wham! Wham! Wham!"—with the bill of a small blue marlin.

"It was incredible," Cassady said. "We never expected a marlin to be so close to shore, and we especially never thought one would hit my tiny wahoo jig."

The marlin turned and greyhounded across the surface, jumping more than 20 times before finally sounding into the warm currents of the Sea of Cortez. Cassady clung to the fishing rod. He had no rod belt to cushion the rod butt, which ground painfully into his gut. The dinghy was cramped and wobbly and offered no protection from the sun.

An hour passed. The marlin surfaced a second time and was tiring. Cassady fought steadily, gaining line with each turn of the spool. Soon the anglers were within reach of the leader and could see the lavender hue beneath the boat.

"It was eerie," Cassady said. "The marlin seemed to look right into my eyes. I got scared for the first time and realized how vulnerable we were. The marlin had pulled us five or six miles from shore, and the wind was picking up. The sea was getting rough and every wave felt big."

But the fear quickly faded. The marlin dashed away, stripping line from the reel. Cassady leaned against the weight, squinting his eyes under the Mexican sun. His muscles ached. It seemed hopeless to try and land a marlin from such a flimsy boat. Fuel, weather and especially drinking water were mounting concerns. Then the line went slack.

Cassady was disheartened. He reeled frantically, hoping the marlin had only changed course. Suddenly the surface erupted in a spray of water. It was the marlin, still hooked and heading straight for the dinghy.

"His tail was all we could see," Cassady said. "It was moving so fast that it looked like the spray from a motorboat. I knew we were in trouble and yelled for Bill to watch out."

The marlin charged. Cassady and Hannah ducked. Huddled together, they covered their heads with their arms, expecting the marlin to leap over the dinghy. But the marlin never left the water.

"When I felt the impact," Cassady said, "I didn't know what to expect. I looked up and saw the marlin thrashing around. His bill was stuck in the side of the dinghy and he couldn't get free. We were taking in a lot of water and losing air fast."

Hannah reached out and gripped the marlin by the bill, gaffing him in the flank with a small hand gaff. The marlin bucked and shook the dinghy violently. Cassady scrambled for an oar and in a desperate attempt to save their lives began beating the marlin over the head.

"I was totally panicked," Cassady said. "We were miles from shore and I'd seen a lot of sharks around. It was life or death as far as I was concerned."

The marlin stopped thrashing, and Cassady laid down the oar. Air rushed from the gash in the side of the dinghy. Hannah stuffed his fingers into the hole. They slid the marlin into the boat and steered for shore.

The rubber gunwale was just above water level when the dinghy streaked into the bay and onto the beach. A crowd of campers gathered around them. The fish was hauled to a nearby tree and hung from a limb for photographs. The catch, a small blue marlin, was estimated to weigh 150 pounds.

"To me it seemed like the biggest marlin in the world," Cassady says.

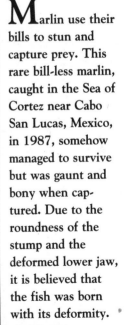

Marlin use their bills to stun and capture prey. This rare bill-less marlin, caught in the Sea of Cortez near Cabo San Lucas, Mexico, in 1987, somehow managed to survive but was gaunt and bony when captured. Due to the roundness of the stump and the deformed lower jaw, it is believed that the fish was born with its deformity.

Courtesy Bernabe Carrizosa Reyes

CAUGHT BELOW THE BELT

I met Capt. Laurie Woodbridge on the deck of his 40-foot sportfisher, Sea Baby II, in Cairns, Australia, in May of 1989. It was off season, and the wharf was peaceful and quiet.

We talked about his unbeaten 1,347-pound world record—a black marlin caught by angler Morton May on 80-pound test. He told me of the year he captured 15 granders, weighing in nine. That was the same year a 1,287-pound black marlin speared his boat, drilling a hole through the lower transom. As the boat began to sink, Woodbridge's deckie shoved a broom handle into the hole. They saved the boat—and landed the fish.

But Woodbridge's favorite story is the one about the novice angler from America whose first fight with a large black marlin nearly cost him his manhood.

"Our angler was an American bloke who'd never caught a big fish in his life and didn't know what to expect. We were in the familiar areas, looking for his first marlin, when the port rigger snapped and our fish was on. Sitting in the fighting chair, harnessed and all clipped in, the angler was watching the marlin jump across the water when it changed course and came toward the boat.

"The fish had slowed down and was underwater,

so I backed the boat up very gently to let the angler get a closer look at him. Leaning forward, the angler grabbed the foregrip of the rod and began to angle it like a light-tackle fisherman. Nobody saw him do it, and the harness began to slip up from under his bum and work its way up and across the top of his back.

"The leader was almost out of the water when the angler jerked the rod a couple of times, spooking the fish. (Keep in mind that the rod is locked into the gimbal on the chair between the angler's legs, and the harness, which is now well up his back, is locked to the reel, causing him to crouch over the rod.) The fish took off, greyhounding toward the horizon. There were 45 pounds of strike drag on the line, and the fisherman wasn't ready for it when it came tight.

"Things happened rather quickly. The rod jerked forward and slammed down over the transom railing, and the angler, with his hand wrapped around the foregrip, followed, letting out a scream as his feet came off the footrest of the chair.

"One second he was sitting up, the next he was lying horizontal across the top of the rod, parallel to the deck and straddling the reel, his hands flailing in the air as he tried to regain his balance.

"The fish was ripping the line off the reel at a blistering pace, and the angler, wearing nothing but his underpants because of the heat that day, lay helplessly over the scorching reel. The spinning line quickly burned through the fork of his pants, and we heard another chilling scream.

"The crewman tried desperately to get the reel to release the drag, but the angler had it covered completely with his body. Luckily the fish stopped its run, and the angler was pushed back into the chair. A detailed check of his anatomy followed, revealing some painful marks but no real damage.

"We settled down to a lengthy fight and finally managed to tag and release the 800-pound marlin— a catch that angler will surely never forget."

BLUEFISH ATTACK

"Be careful!" Dean Toney's mother yelled as she watched her son charge the water at Haulover Beach in Florida.

Ten-year-old Toney waved back, still running full stride. He splashed into the shallow water and dug his toes into the sand. Other children cluttered the shore, and beyond them surfers sat on their boards scanning the horizon for the next set of waves.

Toney felt a rock with his toes and knelt down to grab it when something brushed his leg. He jerked upright and saw a school of mullet darting hither and thither.

"It was great," explained Toney, now 27. "The mullet were everywhere. I started using my shirt as a net, scooping them up and throwing them onto the beach."

Toney's mother also noticed the school of mullet. Concerned, she hurried to the nearest lifeguard stand.

Toney was still catching mullet when another school of fish swam by. These fish were larger and faster than the mullet, and Toney tried to catch them, too.

"I reached down into the water to try and get one," Toney said, "and he bit my finger. He actually swallowed the whole thing. I jerked my hand away, but the fish held on. He was two or three feet long, and finally he flew off my finger toward the beach. I remember looking down at my hand and seeing blood. Then I saw my finger. It was dangling by a thread."

Panic quickly swept the beach as the bluefish, frenzied by the large school of mullet, attacked everything in their path. Frightened children splashed toward the beach while the piranha-like fish nipped at their legs. Even the surfers were attacked by the ferocious feeders.

"There were some ladies standing near the water," Toney said, "and they ran down and wrapped my hand in a towel. Then the lifeguard took me up to the main station. He laid me on a stretcher with another kid until the ambulance arrived."

Toney was taken to Parkway General Hospital, where doctors stitched the finger back to his hand. He spent a week in the hospital and returned for countless surgeries. Although it had been completely severed, the finger healed completely.

Eleven young bathers were attacked that morning at Haulover Beach. One 14-year-old received more than 50 stitches in her lower leg. A 13-year-old boy needed 20 stitches to close his wounds.

It was a day no one ever expected. A day most would like to forget.

DID YOU KNOW?

The more forked the tail fin, the less the water resistance . . . the less the water resistance, the faster the speed. Such is the explanation for the sickle-shaped tail fins of the fastest swimmers.

DANGEROUS OCCUPATION

I n 1976 prominent big game fisherman Bobby Brown was skippering the 37-foot Merritt *No Problem* out of Kona, Hawaii. The ocean was rough with waves measuring three to four feet and rising. The angler on board had been fighting a potential world record blue marlin for more than an hour on 20-pound line before the deckhand had his first opportunity at the leader.

Brown had the boat in reverse and was backing down on the fish when the deckhand wrapped the wire leader around his palm. But before he could take a second wrap, a large wave hit the boat, lift-

ing it up and pulling the wire leader tight against the fish.

The marlin felt the sudden pressure and lunged away with a powerful slap of its tail. The wire tightened around the deckhand's hand and jerked him over the stern into the sea.

"It all happened so fast," Brown said, "that the deckhand never had a chance."

> **❝As the sharp prong pierced the skin, the startled fish sprang high into the air and crashed down inside the cockpit.❞**

Both engines were in full reverse when the deckhand disappeared into the propeller wash. Brown immediately thrust the engine levers forward to full speed. The boat paused, then lunged ahead.

"There was no way for him to avoid those props," Brown said. "It was a vacuum down there in the wash. I just waited for the bloody mess to appear."

But no blood surfaced. Instead, about 30 yards in front of the boat arose a startled deckhand. Somehow the props had missed him. The burst of bubbles from the rapid change of gears had pushed him down and below the churning blades.

"The first thing I noticed was the blue boat paint all over him," Brown said. "He'd slid beneath the props and bounced along the bottom of the boat."

A bewildered and blue deckhand was helped aboard, badly shaken but not injured. The fish was still hooked, and after another hour and a half it finally broke the line.

"We lost the fish," Brown said, "but at least we saved a deckhand."

The following year, Brown was again out fishing from the helm of *No Problem*. This time two of his deckhands were preparing to tag a 200-pound black marlin. One deckhand held the wire leader as the other reached out with the tag stick. But as the sharp prong pierced the skin, the startled fish sprang high into the air and crashed down inside the cockpit.

"All I could see from the bridge was the tail sticking out from the cabin," Brown said.

The marlin was lying across the ice box, his tail draped over the cockpit and his head resting on a bunk inside the cabin. One deckhand was momentarily pinned beneath the marlin; the other, still holding the wire leader, had been knocked into a corner.

Before the marlin had a chance to wreak havoc inside the boat, both deckhands were on their feet and flipped the fish out of the boat and into the water.

But the wire man was still holding the leader in his hand, and overboard he went—again. It was the same deckhand who had survived the deadly propellers a year earlier.

"This time," Brown said gratefully, "the engines were in neutral."

ONE STRONG FISH...
BEACHED BY A
TRAFFIC LIGHT

Capt. Ed Murray, giant tuna fisherman extraordinaire, has witnessed many fishing oddities in his years at the helm of fishing boats. Some were firsthand experiences while others were relayed by radio.

"During the tuna season a few years ago," Murray said, "we heard a report of a hook-up over the radio. It was from a group of fun-loving fisher-men, the nicest bunch you'd ever like to meet, who had never caught a tuna despite years of fishing. They always seemed to get into some kind of trouble, whether it was getting lost, getting their lines tangled up or something of the sort."

Murray's wayward fishermen were fishing in dense fog off Montauk, New York, when a fishing reel clattered with the pull of a forceful fish. One of the anglers removed the fishing rod from its holder, set the hook and began to fight the fish.

"The visibility was less than 100 feet at the time," Murray said, "so we radioed back to confirm their location."

Murray's boat was equipped with a radar system that reported the locations of all incoming radio transmissions. When the tuna-fighting crew reported their location, Murray's radar showed them to be miles from where they reported. Murray was accustomed to the group's ability to get lost, and he quickly radioed back the correction.

"They thought they were 15 miles southeast of Montauk," Murray said, "but my instruments were showing them to be 12 miles northeast. They were lost, but they told me they didn't care. They had finally hooked their big tuna."

Murray monitored the boat's location and continued to fish. Hours later the fog cleared and the anglers reported their catch.

"After fighting for four hours," Murray said, "the tide changed and these guys discovered that their fish was not a tuna. It was a buoyed lobster pot they had snagged in the fog."

Another unusual occurrence recounted by Murray involved a separate group of fishing acquaintances equally prone to trouble.

The fishermen were returning late one evening from the fishing grounds near Montauk. The group was weary and far from home as they approached Freeport, Long Island. They turned toward shore, deciding to dock for the night and resume the trip back the next morning.

"They were nearing their destination," Murray said, "when the chief navigator spotted the first green light marking the passage into port. He soon found the red light that marked the other side of the channel, then another green light, and so on."

The navigator carefully aligned the colored entrance markers and directed the boat toward the center of the channel. The exhausted party of anglers gladly anticipated a calm night's rest inside the harbor when the boat suddenly lurched, grating to a discomfiting stop. The startled crew looked through the darkness and saw surfcasters standing on a beach. The red and green lights were traffic lights along a road that paralleled the shoreline.

DID YOU KNOW?

The longest time at large for a tagged shark is 25 years. The female sandbar shark was tagged in Virginia in 1965 and recaptured 25 years later in Florida. This shark, known for its particularly slow growth, grew an average of one inch per year.

BULL'S-EYE

The Mexican *panga* moved forward slowly, its captain alert for signs of fish. Joan Aubin and her fiancé, Greg Lyznicki, sat on the center thwart scanning the wake, awaiting a strike. It was late in December, 1988, and the East Cape swarmed with game fish.

Suddenly, a glint of silver flashed off to the side of the *panga*. Aubin glimpsed the reflection and was turning to look when the silvery free-jumping wahoo slammed into her head, knocking her unconscious.

"Next thing I knew," Aubin said, "Greg was picking me up from the floor of the boat and my head was pounding."

Her head was also bleeding. The fishing lines were retrieved, and the captain returned to shore.

"Joan was pretty shaken up," Lyznicki said. "The wahoo had jumped at full speed, knocking her clear off the center seat. It glanced off her head and ricocheted into the water."

Once on the beach, Aubin inspected her cuts and bruises. She returned to her hotel, and her head slowly cleared.

The next day, after a night of rest, she boarded a larger boat and landed her first wahoo—a near-record fish caught the traditional way, on rod and reel.

Courtesy Greg Lyznicki

Joan Aubin (right), with help from Dave Lyznicki and his wife Noreen, holds her first wahoo, a 92-pounder. It was a celebrated catch since one day earlier, while fishing from a panga, a smaller free-jumping wahoo had hit her in the head and knocked her unconscious.

WHAT GOES UP MUST COME DOWN

George Williams and Tommy Thompson, both members of the Southern California Tuna Club, were fishing off Dana Point one summer when a marlin they had hooked did the unexpected.

"Tommy hooked the marlin the minute his bait hit the water," Williams said. "But the fish only jumped once and then came straight to the boat. I wanted no part of a green billfish, so I drove forward and had Tommy work on him some more."

The marlin, however, refused to fight. It turned and swam directly back to the boat. Williams, still wary of the fish, put the boat in gear and spun out another few hundred yards of line.

"The marlin must have liked us," Williams continued, "because he turned right around and swam back. Tommy had been complaining about my

moving the boat and threatened to throw the gear overboard if I didn't gaff the marlin. I was feeling bad about it myself, so I jumped into the cockpit and readied the gaff.

"As soon as I grabbed the leader, the marlin came to life and jumped straight up out of the water, brushing the side of the boat. He looked like a missile coming out of the ocean. I yelled to Tommy and ducked."

But Thompson didn't duck. Instead, as the marlin went up, he reached out and snatched it by the bill. The momentum and speed of the fish carried him up off the deck and into the air.

"I've seen a marlin jump pretty high," Williams said, "but not with a 200-pound man hanging on. They went at least another six feet off the deck before they crashed down inside the cockpit."

Thompson's shoulder was dislocated and he couldn't move. The marlin, now corralled inside the boat, flopped and thrashed across the deck. Williams ran to Thompson, lifted him by the shirt and dragged him up to the bridge.

"We waited for the fish to calm down," Williams said, "and then headed in. We had to get Tommy to a doctor.

"It wasn't the easiest way to catch a marlin, but it was certainly one of the most memorable."

BUSHWHACKED BY WHALES

Imagine it's your first big game fishing trip. You've just hooked your first marlin, a whopper, and the excitement is breathtaking. Your adrenaline is flowing, your heart is racing, and everyone on board is whooping and hollering in celebration.

You settle in for the fight. You hope nothing goes wrong. The hook, the line, the reel . . . the whales?

It was a warm January day in 1983, and Joe Nangle and his father Paul had chartered a local fishing boat, *E-Ka-Mo-Na*, at Hawaii's Honokohau Harbor just outside Kona.

The skipper, John Llanes, welcomed the two anglers aboard and within the hour was working the usual fishing grounds. The surface was calm when suddenly, 60 yards away, a pod of pilot whales surfaced. The whales were feeding, and Llanes veered to head them off.

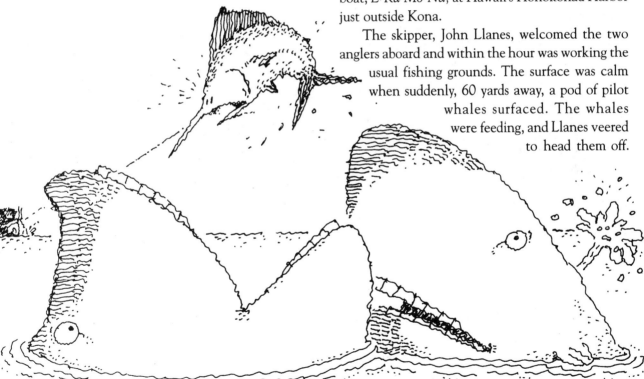

"Marlin!" he shouted from the bridge.

The rod dipped and the engines roared. Nangle leaped into the chair and set the hook on his first marlin—a big one. Her enormous body broke through the surface and soared into the air. She twisted and shook and splashed heavily on the water. She hurled herself upward again and again, each time landing with great force. The captain and crew shouted their approval, estimating her weight at more than 700 pounds. The whales, meanwhile, lolled nearby.

The marlin sounded, and for the next hour Nangle steadily worked the rod, eager to land the trophy fish. The whales continued to linger, docile and seemingly uninterested in the battle. Then suddenly, without warning, they charged.

The exhausted marlin made a desperate plunge for the ocean floor. Line spun from the reel at a blistering pace. The whirling spool became too hot to touch. Nangle watched helplessly as the fishing line he had worked so hard to retrieve faded into blue water. Then it was over. The reel quieted and the line stopped. The marlin had ruptured her air bladder and drowned in the depths.

Relieved to still have weight on his line, Nangle began retrieving his catch. Twenty minutes passed. Then,

DID YOU KNOW?

A great white shark harpooned near Los Angeles in 1976 had not one but two sea lions in its stomach. The first sea lion weighed 175 pounds; the second, 125 pounds.

as the silhouette of the marlin began to emerge, so did the whales. Only this time they were closer.

Nangle reeled frantically with all his strength until the swivel cleared the water. The deckhand reached out, palmed the leader and wrapped it around his hand. He had pulled the marlin within gaffing range when suddenly a huge bull whale appeared beneath the boat. The whale charged the dead marlin, clamping it in its jaws, then turned and raced away from the boat.

The reel spun uncontrollably, and Nangle began to unsnap the harness. But the whale surfaced, stopped swimming and shook the huge marlin in the air like a sardine. Other whales rushed in for the feast, and within seconds Nangle's catch was reduced to blood and foam.

The sound of gunshots filled the air. Fearing for their safety, the captain had fired warning shots to frighten the whales away. Though illegal, the tactic worked and the whales sank below the surface. Quickly, Nangle hauled in what remained of his marlin—180 pounds of head and trailing stomach. The scraps were brought aboard, and Llanes drove ahead at medium speed.

But, like a pack of angry wolves, the whales resurfaced and rushed toward the boat. Unwilling to shoot directly at them, Llanes ordered the marlin head overboard and slammed down the throttles. The boat lurched forward, and as the remnants of Nangle's first marlin faded into the sea, the whales disappeared.

Llanes never slowed his course. Nobody was interested in more fishing.

CAPSIZED CAPTURE

"Mayday! Mayday! We're sinking!" Mele Akaka cried into the radio, straining her eyes toward shore. Volcanic ash from Mauna Loa choked the air, fogging the rocky coastline. "We're five miles from the airport, five miles from the trees on the hill . . . five miles from . . ."

A large wave smashed the side of the 17-foot skiff, shifting Akaka's catch—a 391-pound blue marlin and 100 pounds of *aku*—to one side and flinging Akaka to the deck. Five-foot seas slammed into the stern, sloshing water over the transom. The captain, who had been switching fuel tanks, struggled desperately to connect the fuel hose.

Akaka scrambled to her feet and stared back toward shore. Fear gripped her body. "We were dead in the water," she said afterward, "and the fish in the boat were tilting us to one side. I felt us move backward and looked up to see a huge blue marlin lying on the water. He had one of our lures in his mouth and

was just playing with it. The reel never made a sound. We just started moving backward."

Moving uncontrollably into large waves proved to be a dangerous combination. Before Akaka or the captain could cut the fishing line, the playful marlin changed course, turning the boat sideways into the swells. Seconds later, the skiff capsized.

Capt. Chuck Harlin and his son, Capt. Mike Harlin, were miles away, fishing with clients aboard their 36-foot charter boat *Kealia*. The guests that day were Congressman Joseph Kennedy III of Massachusetts, Congressman Bart Gordon of Tennessee, and two retired football players, John Wilber of the Washington Redskins and Houston Oiler Scott Collins. Also aboard were Kennedy's twin sons, Little Joe and Matthew.

The fishing on the *Kealia* had been slow all morning when Akaka's distress call came over the radio.

"She was understandably frantic," Chuck Harlin said, "and her locations were confusing. She gave three or four different headings. The chances of finding her were pretty remote. We were near one of her locations, and although there was nothing in sight I turned and headed in that direction."

Some time passed before the elder Harlin glimpsed a small white dot on the horizon. He guessed that it was probably nothing more than flotsam, but he veered toward it anyway.

Along the way a fish breached near the flotsam and crashed back into the sea.

66It had been 45 minutes since Akaka's plea for help, and now the rounded frame of the boat bobbed on the surface like the belly of a bloated whale. 99

As the *Kealia* approached, the flotsam gradually grew larger until it became the hull of a small craft. It had been 45 minutes since Akaka's plea for help, and now the rounded frame of the boat bobbed on the surface like the belly of a bloated whale. Two bodies clung desperately to the vertical shaft of the outboard motor.

Mike Harlin, Kennedy and Collins dove into the water and swam to the rescue. They helped Akaka to the *Kealia*, then returned to the overturned boat to survey the damage. Kennedy donned a scuba mask and dove below the surface to try and salvage some gear. Five hundred pounds of dead fish awaited him.

"He nearly walked on water when he saw the dead marlin hanging beneath the boat," Akaka said. "It was the biggest fish he had ever seen, and he was worried about sharks."

Kennedy calmed himself and dove back beneath the boat. A lone rod dangled upside down from the stern, secured to the railing by a safety cord. The limp fishing line trailed out into the blueness. Kennedy unhooked the safety cord and swam the rod and reel to the *Kealia*, where Wilber was waiting.

Wilber began to reel the slack line when unexpectedly it tightened and angled toward the surface. Moments later a blue marlin surged from below, thrashing its head in defiance. The fish that had capsized the boat an hour earlier was still hooked!

Akaka took the rod and tried valiantly to land the fish. But the marlin dove deep, became tailwrapped and died. Wilber also tried to raise the fish, but failed. Finally, Mike Harlin, who had returned from the capsized boat, hand-lined the dead fish to the boat.

Meanwhile, the local boat *Notorious* had arrived and its crew helped right the capsized boat. They tied a rope to the skiff's bow and towed her to harbor. Akaka remained aboard the *Kealia* and returned with her fish and the crew that had saved her life.

CAT FISH

erchel Saxton and Norman Hollingsworth had been fishing together since they were boys. Mostly they fished for bass in the lakes and creeks that abound in Georgia.

The two friends grew older and joined a bass fishing club in the small town of Calhoun. The club organized many annual bass tournaments, and Saxton and Hollingsworth entered them all.

"We were fishing a tournament at Lake Lanier," Saxton said, "and we had gone into one of the small coves to fish for bass along the bank. It was about midnight, and we were using worms."

The two anglers drifted near the shore, eager to hook some of the large bass that hunkered down at night in the shallow water. Hollingsworth carefully soaked his worms in sardine oil before threading them on his hook. It was a technique he had dis-

covered years earlier while snacking on sardines during a slow night of fishing.

"Norm threw out his line, but his worm didn't hit water," Saxton said. "So I said to him, 'You know, you threw your worm up on the bank.' He shook his head and told me he was sure it had hit the water."

Saxton insisted that Hollingsworth's bait was resting on the bank, but Hollingsworth was adamant. Saxton was trying to explain that there had been no splash when Hollingsworth felt a tug on the line.

"I could see a dark object on the bank taking his worm," Saxton said, "but Norm was sure it was a fish. I told him it was probably a raccoon, but he wouldn't listen."

As Hollingsworth jerked his arm to set the hook, the "fish," instead of swimming toward the boat and into deeper water,

traveled away from the boat over the bank. Hollingsworth hollered about a big one and heaved back again on the rod. The "fish" turned and fell from the bank, splashing into the water.

"When the thing fell in the lake," Saxton said, "Norm knew I was right. He didn't have a fish, but he was awfully excited about hooking whatever it was."

Hollingsworth reeled the unidentified creature halfway to the boat, but it splashed back to the bank and up toward the woods. Repeatedly, he pulled it into the water, and each time it scrambled up the bank.

Ten minutes after the strike, the exhausted creature was within view of Saxton's flashlight.

"Damn if it wasn't a cat," Saxton said. "Its eyes were big and yellow, and it was madder than hell. It must have been wild, and Norm wanted me to pull it in the boat. I told him I'd do no such thing and took my knife and cut the line. I wanted no part of an angry alley cat."

Seconds later, the cat scurried over the bank and disappeared into the woods.

"I've fished for 35 years," Saxton said, "and that was the damnedest thing I've ever seen."

LEGENDS, RECORDS AND MYTHS

THE WORLD'S LARGEST STEELHEAD

In the summer of 1970, eight-year-old David White was fishing with his family off Bell Island, Alaska.

"It was around six in the evening," White recalls, "and we were fishing from our inflatable dinghy near the shore," White said. "I had my bait down deep, hoping to catch a giant halibut, but the bait was too close to the bottom and I was constantly getting snagged."

White's dad warned him not to get snagged again. Whenever his line lodged on the bottom, the rest of the family had to reel in their lines and wait while his line was worked free or broken off.

"My dad had already freed up three or four of my snags," White said, "and he told me if it happened again I'd get a spanking. He had me pretty scared, but I put my line down deep anyway."

As the dinghy moved slowly ahead, White's rod slumped over again. "I didn't have my clicker on, so I started letting some line out and hoped my dad wouldn't notice. But he saw what I was doing and his face got red. I knew I was going to get it. I told him I thought it wasn't a snag, but he could see that the line wasn't moving. It was as if I'd hooked onto a piece of lead."

Suddenly White's line swept across the surface of the water. White yelled in excitement. His mom

Courtesy David White

Eight-year-old David White with the largest steelhead ever caught on rod and reel. This all-tackle world record was caught in 1970 and remains unbeaten.

and two brothers reeled in their lines, and his dad shut off the engine. Everyone watched anxiously as the fish raced out a few hundred feet and came to the surface, jumping three or four times in the air.

"When we first saw him," White said, "he was pretty far away and we didn't think he was very big. He was fighting like most of the smaller salmon we were used to catching."

White's dad waited by the engine, ready to follow the fish if necessary. But the fish remained close, and White slowly began to bring in the line. He pulled and reeled and worked the fish toward the boat. But the fish was stronger than most, and each few turns of the reel were soon followed by a blistering run.

"When he was about halfway to the boat," White said, "he jumped again and we saw how big he was. We got really excited then."

The fish charged deep. It came to the surface and sulked. It circled slowly, and took out line in bursts of speed. Then, halfway through the fight, the line suddenly slackened. White reeled frantically.

"I thought for sure he was gone," he said. "But while I was reeling in the line, I saw this shadow under the water. It looked like a submarine coming up. It was a huge fish, and he came up about 10 feet from the boat. The top of his back was almost black, and when he started to move away my line followed him. I couldn't believe how big he was. He was the biggest fish I'd ever hooked."

White reeled with renewed confidence. The fish was tiring, taking less line from the reel with each run. It began to circle near the boat, each turn closer than the previous one. White's dad got the net and waited. He worried about losing the fish by netting too soon. He also worried about his son, who was almost out of strength.

The fish made another slow circle, and White yelled for his dad to net it. He was too tired to continue.

"My dad put the net in the water, and I just sort of guided the fish into it. We learned later that he couldn't see our net. He had lots of scars on his face and had lost an eye. That's probably why we got him so soon."

White's dad quickly slid the netted fish over the side of the boat. The fish flopped about dangerously until White and his brothers could secure it with their legs. They pinned the fish to the floor and gaped in amazement.

It was the most beautiful fish they had ever seen. It had more colors than any salmon they had caught before, and it was huge.

At 10 P.M. the family returned to the dock. White's dad pulled the boat up to the scale and White hauled out his catch. He struggled to lift the fish to his chest as he dragged it to the scale.

"Forty-two pounds, two ounces," the weighmaster announced to the small crowd. White smiled. It was the largest fish he or anyone in his family had ever caught.

The fish was flash-frozen and sent to a taxidermist in White's hometown of Seattle. It was there that the fish was identified as a steelhead. It was the largest one the taxidermist had ever seen. It would soon be a new world record.

"When they first told me it was a steelhead, I didn't really care," White said. "I just cared about catching such a big fish. But when I learned it was a world record, I think I was the happiest kid around." White is now 31 years old, and the steelhead he caught in 1970 remains the all-tackle world record.

MYSTERIOUS GIANT SEA HORSE

Capt. John Vitalich began his career in 1929 as a professional skipper aboard the private yacht *My Oh My*, docked in Avalon Bay, Catalina Island, California. Eventually, he traveled the world in search of game fish, including a memorable season in Tahiti skippering for the legendary Zane Grey.

Vitalich has witnessed many peculiar sights in his years on the sea, but none more puzzling than what he saw as a young boy in the waters off southern California.

"It was during the late summer of 1927," Vitalich said, "and I was fishing for albacore with my father in the channel between San Clemente and Catalina. I was 14 years old and excited to be out fishing. It was midday and flat calm. The fish had quit biting, so we stopped the boat and were just drifting around."

The month was September, and the California weather was warm. Vitalich's father descended to the salon for a nap. Vitalich remained on deck, watching for signs of fish and approaching boats.

"My father hadn't been asleep for more than 10 minutes," Vitalich said, "when a huge mammal surfaced about 75 yards to port. I knew it wasn't a sea lion or an elephant seal because I'd seen them before. This mammal had large eyes and small ears, a long neck and a head much like a horse. It was glossy black and heavy at the shoulders."

Vitalich hollered for his father, who hurried to the deck. "Oh, that's nothing but a sea horse," he told his son. "He won't bother you. I saw one just like that a couple of years ago off the east end of San Clemente. He'll watch us for a while and then sink out of sight."

The odd-looking animal curiously observed the two fishermen, then disappeared beneath the water. Vitalich returned to his watch.

DID YOU KNOW?

The remora is so stubborn, its grip so strong, that many fisherman have used it to catch— or rather, stick to— prey. For example, native Cubans, upon sighting a turtle, would lasso a remora by its tail and toss it overboard. Desperately needing a host, the remora would dart after the turtle and latch on. The fisherman would wait a few seconds, then retrieve his remora and his catch.

A few years passed, and in the early 1930s Vitalich and his friend Loren Grey were passengers aboard the trans-Pacific ship S.S. Manganui. They were sailing from San Francisco to Tahiti, on their way to join Loren's father.

During the voyage, Grey met the diva who was singing in the opera being performed on board. He told her about the blue marlin fishing in Tahiti, and the diva described an unusual creature she had seen while aboard a ferry boat in San Francisco. She told Grey that a large horselike animal surfaced near the boat. Several other people had seen it, she said, and nobody could figure out what it was.

Later that night, Grey related the story to Vitalich.

"Loren was astonished," Vitalich recalled. "Years earlier, when I'd told him about my sighting of the sea horse off Catalina Island, he just shook his head in disbelief. But when he heard the diva describe the same animal, he knew there was something to it."

Vitalich never heard of nor saw the mysterious sea horse again. Sixty years later, however, the image remains vivid in his mind.

"The animal seemed almost friendly," he said, "as if it wanted to stay and watch us but was too afraid. I don't know what it was, but I know it was there.

"I've spent a lifetime on the water, and nothing surprises me much anymore."

MONSTROUS HALIBUT

It was a pleasant summer day in Tutka Bay, Alaska, 15 miles across from Kachemak Bay near the city of Homer. Glenda Rosenbalm and her husband Bill loaded their 18-foot fishing boat for a short but leisurely fishing tour around the bay. Along for the tour were Bill's relatives, Ed and Kathy Hodgson.

Glenda, who planned to return within the hour, left a chicken cooking in the oven. Neither she nor Bill brought along a gun, something they always did when halibut fishing.

"We were just excited to get on the water," Glenda recalled. "Kathy and Ed were anxious to see the bay, and we weren't going out for long. The fishing was just a last-minute thought."

Once on the bay, Bill stopped the boat and set the anchor. The fishing lines were baited and lowered to the sandy floor 70 feet below. When 30 minutes passed without a strike, the group decided to head back for supper. Glenda picked up her six-foot fishing rod strung with 80-pound line and pulled back. The rod bowed forward and the line didn't move.

"I thought I was snagged," Glenda said. "I was trying to decide what to do when I felt a funny movement on the pole. I pulled again, but still nothing happened. It was just like pulling on the side of a barn."

As she turned to ask Bill for help, the line moved. She held the rod steady, felt another movement and heaved back.

"I knew then that I wasn't snagged," Glenda continued, "because I felt movement. It wasn't much, but it was enough to keep me interested."

The hooked halibut hardly moved, and at 6:30 that evening Glenda was still pulling. She had managed to raise the fish one time, but only briefly and only about three feet from the bottom. The halibut hovered for an instant, then settled back into its hole. Bill never had to raise the anchor.

Some commercial boats were anchored nearby, awaiting the following day's opening of salmon season. Soon aware of Glenda's predicament, they called her by radio to offer assistance and support.

"I remember one of the fellas on a commercial boat asking about a gun. When we told him ours was at home, he brought over a little .22-caliber rifle. An hour later, he came back with a .30-.30."

The fish still hadn't moved and Glenda was exhausted. Reluctantly she passed the rod to Ed, who beamed with confidence. He accepted the rod and pulled with all his strength, to no avail.

Ed persisted, and during the next hour and a half the fish surfaced once and then settled back

> **"The halibut that began as a snag measured almost eight feet from nose to tail."**

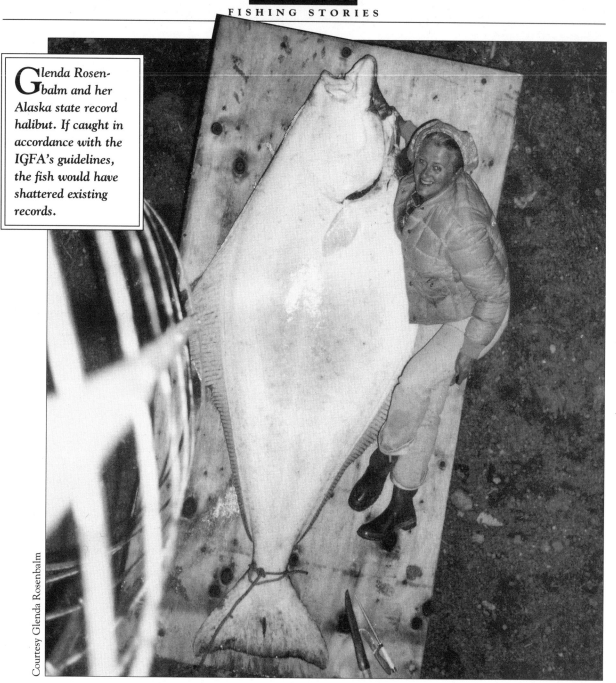

Glenda Rosenbalm and her Alaska state record halibut. If caught in accordance with the IGFA's guidelines, the fish would have shattered existing records.

Courtesy Glenda Rosenbalm

into its hole. It was a big fish, the largest halibut they had ever seen.

The Alaskan sky turned to an eerie dusk that would last the night. Ed worked diligently, but as the hours passed, the mood on board turned to frustration. Glenda, who felt responsible for the catch, announced a new and desperate strategy. She told Ed to tighten the drag and crank in the line. The fish could do what it wanted.

"It was a funny thing," Glenda said. "That great big halibut came straight up without a fight. She must have been really tired. She got to the top of the water and just laid there."

Ed held the line steady while the commercial fisherman with the .30-.30 took aim and ended the fight. The halibut was towed and then hoisted from the rigging of a nearby commercial boat. Glenda watched in disbelief. The halibut that began as a snag measured almost eight feet from nose to tail. It was four feet wide and a foot and a half thick.

After some well-deserved victory beers aboard the commercial boat, Bill tied the fish to their small boat and the weary crew returned home. It was well after midnight when they arrived. The chicken dinner was more than cooked, but nobody minded.

The next morning, it took Glenda and Ed seven hours to butcher the monster halibut. They carved more than 200 pounds of fillets and roasts from the body of the fish. Each cheek, considered a delicacy, weighed a pound and a half.

Glenda removed the 50-pound halibut head and took it to the local Fish and Game Department. The otolith bone was removed from the fish's ear and sent to the Seattle Halibut Commission for tests. The results concluded that the halibut was a female, age 30.

The Fish and Game Department used the halibut's measurements to calculate a weight of 450 pounds. If it had been caught within the International Game Fish Association's guidelines, the fish would have set a world record.

"We never thought about world records during the fight," Glenda said. "If we knew how big she was going to be, we never would have shot her and I never would have given up the rod."

Though not recognized as a world record, the catch did qualify for the Alaskan state record. It remains unbeaten.

DID YOU KNOW?

A confrontation with a giant squid left sucker wounds 18 inches in diameter (nearly twice the size of a basketball) on the body of a large sperm whale. Scientists who studied the dead whale estimated the squid's length to be an astonishing 200 feet.

36-TO-1 WITH A GRANDER

In 1983, Rinaldo Wenk caught a 626-pound blue marlin on 30-pound test line. It was a 20-to-1 world record thought by many to be unbeatable. Then, on a midsummer day in Kona, Hawaii, the record was shattered by more than 470 pounds.

June 25, 1987, was the first day of a new moon. Capt. Kelley Everette and his three-man crew fired up the twin diesels of the 37-foot Merritt *Northern Lights*, hoping to land a record marlin on light tackle.

> **"She's huge!" he screamed as the marlin cleared the water for the third time. "She's huge!"**

Everette was in the cockpit that morning. He was replacing his wife Jocelyn, who was recovering from a difficult marlin battle the day before.

Carl Sloder, Everette's first mate, was at the helm. Scott Davidson, the gaff man, and Dominic Fredundes, the leader man, were in the cockpit with Everette.

By midmorning the crew had lost one marlin at the strike and had returned to the bait buoy. They caught a small *aku* and were preparing to return to the site of the earlier strike when Fredundes sensed that a fish was near. He rigged the *aku* and set it out 30 fathoms from the stern, holding the line in his hand rather than clipping it into the outrigger.

On the second lap around the buoy, the bait began to jerk sporadically. Fredundes' eyes narrowed and fixed on the fishing line.

"We were anxious," Everette remembers. "We knew Dominic had felt something unusual, and we knew that look in his eyes meant a strike was coming."

Quickly, Fredundes sprang back and released the line. The backdrop sliced through the water. Sloder reversed the engines and Everette fed out line.

At the count of 10, Sloder slammed the throttles forward. The rod slumped over and line tumbled from the spool. The marlin did not jump, descending instead into the strong currents below.

"Stay with her!" Everette yelled. "She's big!"

Two hours passed. They knew the marlin was large, but was it a record? Everette worked the drag, pressing it forward until the line pinged. Any more pressure and it would snap.

Finally the swivel broke the surface. Everette locked the drag, and Fredundes reached for the leader.

But just before it came within gaffing range, the marlin slapped its tail in a sudden dash for freedom.

"It happened so fast," Everette said. "The drag was locked, and I was sure the line would snap."

But the marlin didn't sound and the line held. Everette flipped the drag into free-spool and waited. The fish ruptured the surface and soared into the air, burning Everette's thumb as he tried to slow the free-spooling reel.

"She's huge!" he screamed as the marlin cleared the water for the third time. "She's huge!"

Sloder reversed the boat full speed. The marlin was swimming on the surface, too tired to sound. Everette reeled frantically to keep the line taut as wave after wave crashed over the transom and onto the deck.

The marlin descended portside, then surfaced starboard. Fredundes lunged at the leader, grabbed it in his left hand and took a quick double wrap. He pulled the line to his chest and wrapped it again, then again. The marlin was just within range and Davidson lunged with the gaff, digging it deep into the fish.

It was a perfect shot but not enough to slow the fish. It crossed under the boat and surfaced portside. Davidson rushed across the deck and sank two more gaffs into the wide flank.

The massive fish shook with fury, tearing away from the boat at blazing speed. Suddenly, a loud *pop!* cracked the air. The leader had snapped.

All that held the fish were the three gaff ropes. They stretched like rubber bands, the strain tremendous, when two gaffs ripped free and flung back toward the boat. Both hooks whizzed past Davidson and Fredundes at deadly speed.

Capt. Kelley Everette (far right) and his fishing crew—Carl Sloder (far left), Scott Davidson (front left) and Dominic Fredundes (front right)—with their record-shattering catch.

Courtesy Capt. Kelley Everette

Davidson wrestled the remaining gaff rope and held it tightly. Everette took the lower controls and yelled for Sloder to get another gaff. Sloder jumped from the bridge, and two more gaffs were quickly sunk into the fish. But the marlin didn't stop. It fought furiously, pulling out another gaff and dragging the boat backward.

"It was incredible," Everette said. "I'd never seen anything like that in my life. Water was pouring over the transom and into the deck as Carl followed in reverse."

Davidson gaffed the marlin for the sixth time and cleated the rope to the boat. Finally, the marlin slowed. Fredundes reached out beyond the covering board and took the fish by the bill while Everette and Davidson held his legs and watched.

> **❝The marlin didn't stop. It fought furiously, pulling out another gaff and dragging the boat backward.❞**

"It took Dominic 10 minutes," Everette said, "with Carl's help, to subdue the fish. It took that much time before we felt it was safe to bring her inside the cockpit. I never thought she would fit, but she did."

The exhausted crew pulled the marlin through the transom door and into the cockpit. It was as long as the cockpit and measured three feet high. Without warning, it began thrashing and sent the bewildered crew for cover.

"When she finally stopped, I knew it was over," Everette said. "Dominic looked like he had just won an Olympic gold medal. We were hugging and jumping up and down. We knew we had a world record, but we didn't know by how much."

Back at the dock, rumors of the world record spread. Capt. Phil Parker, a well-known local skipper and International Game Fish Association representative, was the weighmaster that day. He watched as the fish was raised to the scale. "The men's world record," he called out to the crowd, "on 30-pound test, is 628 pounds."

Parker climbed the scale ladder and placed the register on 628 pounds, but the bar didn't move. The crowd celebrated. Slowly, Parker moved the register in 100-pound increments until it reached 1,028 pounds. Still no movement.

"It's a grander!" Parker shouted to the roaring crowd. He eased the weight another 100 pounds and the bar flipped to the top. He lowered the weight back down and it leveled at 1,103 pounds. The crowd erupted with excitement. No one had ever landed a grander on 30-pound test. It was a first in fishing history.

Champagne flowed and leis were passed around. The previous record had been nearly doubled. Not only was Everette's marlin the largest ever caught on 30-pound test; it was also the largest marlin ever caught on all but the heaviest tackle allowed by the International Game Fish Association.

That night Everette knelt beside his bed and said a quick prayer. He had lost a leg 10 years earlier, an injury many considered a handicap. "I never thought about it that way," he said. "I kept my faith in God and worked as hard as I could.

"It was a great accomplishment to catch that fish, and there are those who say this record will never be beaten—but that's what they said about the last one."

THE UFO AND THE BROADBILL

"What in the blimin' hell is that!" an anxious voice cried over the radio.

A calm sea gently rocked the smattering of drifting fishing boats.

"What's buggerin' you, mate?" replied Capt. Bruce Smith from the bridge of his charter boat *Lady Doreen*. It was nighttime, and Smith, one of New Zealand's most respected big game captains, was fishing for swordfish outside the Bay of Islands. Two anglers slept on the lower deck and two fishing rods rigged with squids angled from the stem.

The voice returned. "Don't you see it? Toward the shore, just left of Matehei Bay!"

Smith stood and turned toward shore. A huge bank of flashing lights hovered in the distance. "No

Courtesy Bernabe Carrizosa Reyes

This sea monster washed ashore three miles north of Cabo Can Lucas in 1973. One of the most puzzling aspects of the mysterious creature was the hairy skin that covered its body. It also had an obvious whale-like tail and backbone but no protruding limbs. The anomaly was discovered by local residents on a remote beach, and no physical remains exist.

worries, mate," he reported back. "It's just some blimin' commercial liner with its deck lights on."

The lights began to quiver. They seemed to shudder and whirl in place, then accelerated along the coast at a terrific rate of speed, past Takau Bay and down toward Rocky Point, miles away.

Smith watched the blur of speeding lights drop low on the horizon and disappear in a red pulsating glow. "Christ, mate! Did you see that?" he stammered into the radio.

"Yeah . . ." was the only reply.

The red glow faded into darkness, and soon the calm of the night had returned. Glad to be rid of the lights, Smith sat back and concentrated on the fishing lines.

Suddenly, the sky lit up again. Smith jumped from his seat and saw that the same flashing lights had returned. "They're comin' right for us!" he yelled. "If it's a boat, they'll ram us!"

The lights zoomed toward the *Lady Doreen*, just above the water. They fluttered as they approached, then separated into windows. Smith, still certain that the mysterious lights were from the deck of a speeding ship, screamed for his deckie to shine a spotlight into the lights.

"Maybe they don't see us!" he yelled.

The deckie turned the spotlight into the sky and the mass of speeding lights vanished. Smith checked his radar screen. Nothing. He called the captain of the *Aquarius*, who had first reported the strange lights.

"Nothing's showing on my radar, either," the skipper said uneasily. "That sure as hell wasn't a boat."

It was just after midnight, but it seemed much later. No one slept that night, and the eerie lights never returned. No fish were caught, and by early dawn the skippers had turned their boats toward home, glad the night was over.

THE BIG ONE

Capt. George "The Fox" Bransford had retired from big game fishing by the time I drove down his driveway in central Queensland, Australia. Originally from Florida, Bransford had spent a lifetime as a professional skipper, fishing much of the world. "The Fox" was a legend now. He had been for a long time.

The successful capture of Australia's first grander began by chance during World War II. Bransford was an American paratrooper stationed in the small town

Courtesy Cairns Game Fishing Club

Capt. George Bransford (left) and Richie Obach with the fish that put Australia on the sport fishing map. The 1,064-pound black marlin was the first Australian grander ever caught on rod and reel.

of Gordonville on the northeastern coast of Australia. From training missions high above the sea, he began to study the Great Barrier Reef.

A fisherman by trade, Bransford was intrigued by the stark blue line that marked the edge of the great reef. It was there, he believed, that the warm currents of the ocean would mix with the rich waters of the reef, creating ideal conditions for game fish . . . lots of them.

> **66It was a day free of charters, a day for exploring new ground. Their destination was the edge of the reef, the continental shelf, more than 30 miles from the coast.99**

At every opportunity he went to the seaside town of Cairns, where the reef was nearest to shore. He watched the local mackerel boats return from fishing, and he talked with their captains. They all complained about the same thing: big menacing fish that attacked their mackerel.

It was just what Bransford was looking for, and he decided to return one day to pursue a dream.

The year was 1964, 20 years after the young paratrooper had vowed to return to Cairns. He began searching the inner reefs for billfish, but the fishing was slow. Bransford had sold his home in the States, moved his family and staked it all on finding these fish. He needed results.

Late that year, on November 25, he caught a 35-pound black marlin. Then in early 1965 his wife Joyce caught the largest marlin ever landed in Australia, a 252-pound black marlin. The catch was enough to keep a local interest in their budding charter business, the first of its kind along the coast.

On September 28, 1965, almost a year after landing his first black marlin, Bransford and his deckie, Richie Obach, navigated their way toward the outer waters far beyond the reef. It was a day free of charters, a day for exploring new ground. Their destination was the edge of the reef, the continental shelf, more than 30 miles from the coast. Fresh baits were rigged and skipped along the water's surface, but by early afternoon the only fish in the box were mackerel, trevally and barracuda.

Then from beneath the water came a huge black bill. "Marlin! Port 'rigger," hollered Bransford. His heart raced as the fish slapped the bait with terrific force. The 80-pound line snapped from the outrigger clip and spun from the reel. The marlin's body shuddered, then disappeared beneath the water.

Immediately the sea erupted. The marlin rocketed from the surface, thrusting its head from side to side to escape the jab of the hook. Repeatedly it charged the surface, and repeatedly the reel shrieked. History was in the making.

Obach held the rod and followed Bransford's commands. He was young and strong, and eager to catch the monster fish.

"Don't let him rest!" Branford yelled. "Give it all you've got and then some . . . More pressure,

Richie—now's when you need to give him hell. Don't give him an inch!"

Together they worked, constantly talking, always alert. It was two hours before the fish tired. Obach pulled one last time and the leader hit the rod tip. He slid the rod into its holder and dug a gaff deep into the fish.

It was big, at least 700 or 800 pounds. They tried to pull it into the cockpit, but its size was too great. Their only choice was to tie it off the stern and tow it to shore.

Night had fallen, so the treacherous trip home had to be navigated by moonlight. Slowly, weaving through the lattice of shallow reefs, they made their way to the dock. It had been two hours since they reported their catch, and a large crowd was waiting. But it was late and the scales were closed. They put the fish in a makeshift freezer. The final weight would be delayed until morning.

At daybreak, the marlin was carted by truck across town to the certified scales located at the railroad station. The crowd had returned and whooped happily as the scales reached 1,064 pounds. It was the first grander ever caught in Australia and a new world record. The black marlin measured nearly 14 feet from bill to tail and had a girth of 81 inches.

His heart raced. The fish was enormous, slapping the bait with terrific force.

The gamble had paid off. Bransford's dream had come true.

THE 1,000-POUNDER AND THE AIRCRAFT CARRIER

I t was a pleasant island morning when I wandered onto Honokohau pier to meet Capt. George Parker, the famed skipper who made billfishing history in 1954 by landing the first 1,000-pound Pacific blue marlin on rod and reel.

He had a half-day charter booked and asked me to go along. After months of research and no fishing, it was a welcome invitation. We motored from the harbor and, after setting the lures, began talking about that historical first grander.

T he year was 1954, and Parker was piloting his 50-foot *Mona H* across the windy strait from his home in Kona, Hawaii. He was headed to a dry-dock facility in Honolulu, on the neighboring island of Oahu.

At 5 o'clock in the afternoon, he passed Koko Head on the way to his destination. He fished three lures he had made from shiny chrome towel racks filled with a wooden core and fitted with red automobile inner tubes cut to resemble squid legs. Two sharpened hooks dangled beneath each of the homemade skirts.

Happy to be fishing, Parker let his attention shift to a nearby aircraft carrier whose pilots were practicing takeoffs and landings from the large, flat deck. "I forgot about fishing," he recalled. "I was too intrigued by the Navy's exercises on that carrier. Then, all of a sudden, one of the reels went off. I ran back and pulled in my other two lines, leaving the boat going full speed ahead."

Losing line fast, Parker carried the bent rod forward to the controls. "As I went to pull the throttle back, the fish jumped at least 100 yards ahead of me. He had made a U-turn and just passed me up. That's when I saw how big he was."

Parker knew he had to straighten the line, but the boat responded too slowly. He put the boat in neutral, loosened the drag and began walking the line around the boat. "The only difficulty," he explained, "other than keeping my balance, was handing the rod from one hand to the other around the cabin struts. Luckily, I only had to make one trip around the boat to clear the line."

The cockpit of the *Mona H* was equipped with a wooden bench with three attached rod sockets. Parker completed his walk around the boat and slid the rod into one of the sockets and began to fight the fish. Then he saw the Navy.

"The aircraft carrier I'd been watching earlier had been joined by a naval destroyer, and the two of them were coming across my stern—close enough to cut my fishing line. I was stuck, and I couldn't do a damn thing about it. I just concentrated on my fish, cursed the Navy and hoped my line was deep enough to miss their propellers."

The Navy, however, was not amused. Its planes were routed to land nearby, and this was no place for a small pleasure craft.

"I heard the Navy radioman call for the area to be cleared," Parker said. "When I didn't move, a chopper was dispatched to fly over and tell me personally to get out of the way. I'll never forget seeing that pilot hovering above me, looking down and laughing at the sight of me stubbornly fighting a fish in their lane."

The helicopter returned to the carrier and the Navy altered its course.

Darkness neared, and the *Mona H* was overdue in Honolulu. The radio crackled with a call from a concerned friend. Parker carried his fishing rod with him, walked to the radio and explained the situation. The friend offered to help and was soon en route with assistance.

"I wasn't that far from Honolulu," Parker said, "but it took an hour and a half for him to reach me. He was using his radio frequency direction finder

Capt. George Parker with the 1,002-pound blue marlin he caught in 1954. It was the first 1,000-pound blue marlin to be caught on rod and reel in the Pacific Ocean.

and having a difficult time pinpointing my location. I had to walk back and forth to my radio, giving him directions while holding the rod between my legs."

By the time his friend finally arrived, Parker had drifted eight miles from the hook-up location to an area off Diamond Head.

"It wasn't until we got to the area near the Royal Hawaiian Hotel," Parker said, "that the marlin began to tire. He circled us for a while before he surfaced. We heard his tail splash the water and shined our flashlights into the darkness. He was upside down and floating on the water. His air sacks were bloated, and I knew from experience that all we had to do was position the boat in the direction he was swimming and he'd swim right to us."

The marlin did more than that. Discombobulated by fatigue, the fish crashed into the stern, sinking its sword into the wooden transom.

Parker set down the rod and gaffed the marlin once on each side. He made a few half hitches around the bill, lashed the fish to the stern and headed for Honolulu.

> **66 The aircraft carrier I'd been watching earlier had been joined by a naval destroyer, and they were coming across my stern— close enough to cut my fishing line. 99**

The marlin was 15 feet long with a girth of 76 inches—so big that they needed a station wagon to hoist it from the boat. But it was late, 9 o'clock on a Saturday evening, and the scales were closed.

The next day, after lying in a reefer box overnight, the marlin was weighed. Having lost an estimated 10% of its weight to dehydration, the fish still weighed an impressive 1,002 pounds. It was a new world record and the first 1,000-pound blue marlin ever landed on rod and reel in the Pacific Ocean. Or so Parker thought.

"Francisca LaMont was the recordkeeper for the International Game Fish Association, and she had just written a book in which she said that no blue marlin lived in the Pacific. She said they live only in the Atlantic, which meant our fish had to be classified as a black marlin. I knew it wasn't a black, but I couldn't change her mind."

Parker persisted. He was certain the fish was a blue marlin, and five years later, after endless debate and correspondence, the IGFA acknowledged the world record under the new heading "Pacific Blue Marlin." The record was retroactive to include the previous 5 years and remained unbeaten for 10 years thereafter.

A WORLD RECORDS DAY

Jack Erskine, owner of the internationally recognized tackle shop that bears his name, was in search of a world record when he left the docks in Cairns, Australia. When he returned later that afternoon, he had four.

"The IGFA," Erskine said, "had just announced the new 2-kilogram-line class for black marlin. Nobody had ever caught a black on such light line, so I called up Capt. Laurie Woodbridge and asked him if he wanted to give it a try."

He did, and the two met on Woodbridge's boat, *Sea Baby II*. Their plan was to troll teaser mullets (hookless baits) on heavy line in hopes of luring the marlin close to the boat. Erskine would wait for the fish to come close, cast out a freshly rigged bait, free-spool the line and try to set the hook. Finally, if all went well, Woodbridge would chase the fish until Erskine recovered the line—without breaking it off.

"Our biggest worry was putting too much pressure on the fish," Erskine recalled. "Two-kilogram line doesn't allow for mistakes. Our other main concern was the leader. Our deckies were expert gaff and wire men, but they wouldn't be able to pull hard on the leader since the fish might not be hooked solidly. Finally, if the deckie missed on the first gaff, we were sure to lose the fish."

The strategy worked, and their performance was nearly flawless. Of the nine fish caught that day, four were boated, three were released and two lost. Remarkably, each fish caught was larger than the previous one, each setting a new world record. The final tally for the day was four world records—all in the same line class.

"It was an incredible day," Erskine said. "We just kept beating our own record."

The first world record fish that day weighed 35 pounds; the last, 45 pounds. Later that year, while fishing off Bribie Island in Queensland, Erskine landed another black marlin, again on 2-kilogram line. The 72-pound, 12-ounce marlin broke Erskine's previous record by nearly 30 pounds and remains unbeaten.

Courtesy Alfred Glassell Jr.

A leap into history. Alfred Glassell Jr.'s 1,560-pound world record black marlin. The fish, caught in 1953, is still the largest world record marlin.

WORLD'S LARGEST FRESHWATER FISH

It was a Saturday morning approaching noon when Joey Pallotta and a friend arrived at the docks in Benicia, California. They bought a scoop of grass shrimp at the local bait shop and boarded Joey's boat, steering west through the Carquinez Strait toward the San Francisco Bay.

"The wind was really blowing on the bay," Pallotta said, "so we turned back into the strait. On our way back I saw a fish jump. The water was pretty deep there and I liked the area, so we anchored down and rigged the shrimps."

Ten minutes passed without any luck. Pallotta's eyes constantly skimmed the water's surface, his view never leaving the rod. As a slight breeze rocked the boat, the rod tip began to bounce gently. It was the pump of a sturgeon strike. Pallotta carefully lifted the rod from the holder and waited.

"He was a suicide fish," Pallotta said. "When I picked up the rod, I expected to wait for the usual third or fourth pump, but this fish immediately pulled straight down."

Pallotta reined back on the rod, digging the hooks deeply into the fish's leathery mouth. The fish hovered near the bottom, then surged upward, splitting the surface scarcely 50 yards away. It thrashed on the surface and then plunged back to the muddy bottom. Palotta worried as the line poured from the spool. "The tide was pulling the fish down the strait and into the bay. We were in trouble, so we cut the anchor rope and went out with him. He was a strong fish, and for the first two hours I never gained any line."

Eventually, the tide shifted and the sturgeon returned to the strait. Pallotta had fought many sturgeons before, but none as powerful as this.

"A good friend of mine, Tom Galakeler, was fishing close by," Palotta said. "His boat was bigger, and he agreed to come help me out."

Other boats drifted nearby, the fishermen hoping to see the monster sturgeon. Pallotta's line began to rise. The fish rushed the surface and jumped a second time. It was enormous.

"After he jumped," Pallotta said, "he really began to fight. He took multiple runs up and down and around the boat. We pulled him toward the shallows and he pulled us toward the bay. Nobody seemed to be winning."

Pallotta's reel began to malfunction. It continued to overheat, forcing him to pour cool water over the spool. Galakeler, meanwhile, did what he could, watching the line and keeping the boat in neutral for the fish to tow.

The sturgeon came to the surface 13 times without confronting the gaff. Then, at 8:15 in the eve-

Joey Pallotta with his record sturgeon, which may remain in the record books forever.

Courtesy Joey Pallotta

ning, the fish surfaced for the 14th and final time.

"He fought hard at the gaff," Pallotta said, "but we held tight. When he stopped splashing, we tied him to the stern. The boat's beam was 12 feet long, and the sturgeon stretched easily from one end to the other."

The record sturgeon was still alive, and the dock was only five minutes away. When he arrived, Pallotta ran to a telephone and called the Steinhart Aquarium. He wanted to save the fish if he could. But the biologist at the Aquarium wasn't interested. Pallotta was forced to make a difficult decision.

> **❝I knew it was a once-in-a-lifetime fish, but part of me wanted to let him go.❞**

"It was a real hard one for me. I knew it was a once-in-a-lifetime fish, but part of me wanted to let him go. He was big and old and had been around for a long time. I'd fished most of my life, and I cared a lot about these fish. I guess I finally decided that I deserved the record, and that I could make this fish live forever."

Pallotta's next call was to the local Game and Fish Department. His record catch needed an accurate weight from a registered scale, but the scale at Benicia measured only to 300 pounds. The Fish and Game representative advised him to take the fish to a certified truck scale in one of the surrounding cities. Pallotta and Galakeler loaded the fish into Galakeler's truck, and by 11 o'clock that evening they were on the road to Fairfield, 45 minutes away. When they arrived, the scales were closed.

They drove to the C&H Sugar Refinery in Crockett, a half-hour drive farther inland. But state health regulations barred weighing fish on their scales.

Frustrated, tired and out of ideas, the two fishermen drove to a friend's house nearby.

"My buddy's wife," Pallotta explained, "knew someone at the Sante Fe Railroad Station. It was 2:30 in the morning by the time she called him, but he agreed to weigh the fish."

After hours of drying in the sultry night air, the fish weighed an impressive 468 pounds. Pallotta and Galakeler placed the fish in a walk-in freezer and waited for daylight.

The next morning the media were notified, and reporters and photographers arrived in droves to meet the local angler responsible for the world's largest freshwater catch.

"We hung the fish on the local scale," Pallotta said, "but it broke. Then everything went wild. Cameras were flashing and everybody was asking me questions. It was really something."

The fish was filleted and the skin stretched and dried for mounting. A mold was made and the first cast hung proudly above Pallotta's fireplace. A huge poster-size photograph was later draped from his living room wall and another in the local bait shop.

Since then, maximum size limits have been set for sturgeon fishing, assuring Pallotta the top spot in the record books. And unless the restrictions change, his fish will, as Pallotta wished, live forever.

A TRIBUTE TO THE FISH

It was not uncommon during my search for fishing stories to hear how extraordinary the fishing used to be. A time when we did not stock lakes and streams with lazy domesticated fish; when acres of marlin sunned lazily atop unpolluted swells; when swordfish were common and tuna a nuisance.

I envy Zane Grey and his boundless trout streams. Ernest Hemingway and his prolific Gulf Stream. I yearn for the days when the fish were too big to catch and too plentiful to plunder.

I have written *Incredible Fishing Stories* as a way to record some of fishing's most extraordinary moments. I have done so, not as an epilogue, but as an introduction. I hope we can end the cycle of telling future generations about the trophy bass that no longer spawn, about the large schools of porpoise that no longer blur the horizon, about the streams and lakes whose fish you could once eat.

Listed here are organizations dedicated to the sport of fishing. Each is important to the preservation of our sport, and all could use your help. I encourage you to join at least one of them. The future of sport fishing depends on it.

Remember, it is not whether you catch the fish, but the stories you can tell at the end of the day.

International Game Fish Association (IGFA)
1301 E. Atlantic Blvd.
Pompano Beach, FL 33060
305-941-3474

The Billfish Foundation (TBF)
2419 East Commercial Blvd.
Suite 303
Ft. Lauderdale, FL 33308
(305) 938-0150

American Sportfishing Association (ASA)
1033 N. Fairfax Street
Suite 200
Alexandria, VA 22314
(703) 519-9691

National Coalition for Marine Conservation
5105 Paulsen St., Suite 243
Savannah, GA 31905
912-354-0441

ACKNOWLEDGMENTS

I am sincerely grateful to all the fishermen who took part in this book. A very special thanks goes to Doug McFetters, Capt. Dennis "Brazakka" Wallace, Capt. Mike "Beak" Hurt, Dr. Hal Neibling, Jim Rizzuto, Terry Snow, Dale Gullicksen, and Mike Leech of the International Game Fish Association. I cannot thank them enough for helping to make *Incredible Fishing Stories* a reality.

I thank Keith Graham of Australia and Malcolm McGeorge of New Zealand for helping me track down stories in countries where I was but an unknown visitor. And to Jared Lee, whose illustrations have added humor and delight, thank you for making this book more enjoyable to us all.

Finally my deepest appreciation goes to my publisher Peter Workman, to my editors Sally Kovalchick and Lynn Strong, and to Paul Hanson for designing the book. From the hearts of fishermen everywhere, thank you.